Willpower

FOR

DUMMIES®

A Wiley Brand

D0825431

Willpower

FOR DUMMIES®

A Wiley Brand

by Frank Ryan

FOR DUMMIES®

A Wiley Brand

Willpower For Dummies®

Published by: **John Wiley & Sons, Ltd.,** The Atrium, Southern Gate, Chichester, www.wiley.com

This edition first published 2013

© 2014 John Wiley & Sons, Ltd, Chichester, West Sussex.

Registered office

John Wiley & Sons Ltd, The Atrium, Southern Gate, Chichester, West Sussex, PO19 8SQ, United Kingdom

For details of our global editorial offices, for customer services and for information about how to apply for permission to reuse the copyright material in this book please see our website at www.wiley.com.

For general information on our other products and services, please contact our Customer Care Department within the U.S. at 877-762-2974, outside the U.S. at (001) 317-572-3993, or fax 317-572-4002. For technical support, please visit www.wiley.com/techsupport.

A catalogue record for this book is available from the British Library.

ISBN 978-1-118-68003-2 (pbk), ISBN 978-1-118-68000-1 (ebk), ISBN 978-1-118-68001-8 (ebk)

Printed in Great Britain by TJ International, Padstow, Cornwall

10 9 8 7 6 5 4 3 2 1

Contents at a Glance

Table of Contents

Introduction

*W*illpower For Dummies was written to enable you make the most of your willpower. The book presents and explains a necessarily wide variety of information and diverse strategies aimed at helping you manage your willpower efficiently. Whether you're concerned with engaging your willpower to suppress an unwanted habit such as smoking or gambling, or you've concluded that lack of willpower is preventing you from reaching your full potential at school, university or work, this book has something for you. This book provides you with the latest and best ideas and tools for maximising your willpower.

The central theme of the book is that willpower relies on a set of core skills you can learn and improve through practice. With the skills I impart here, you can realise your dreams and conquer unwanted habits.

But don't worry, the book isn't a willpower boot camp! Enhancing your willpower often involves making small, sometimes surprisingly obvious, changes to your daily routine and mindset. These small steps help create an environment in which your willpower can flourish throughout the years to come. Kindness to yourself and others also matters a lot.

Last but by no means least, willpower is, to a great extent, a reflection of brain power. I don't mean that you have to be clever to develop your willpower. Far from it. Willpower isn't that closely related to intelligence (but is a better predictor of success and achievement through a person's lifespan). What I do mean is that using willpower, particularly in overcoming impulses or temptations, but also in maintaining goals, works best if you have a healthy, well-nourished and fit brain. All is revealed in the willpower workshop!

About This Book

Willpower For Dummies is full of useful information, tips and checklists to help you better understand and utilise your willpower.

Perhaps you bought this book because you believe that you lack willpower. You're not alone. In fact, everybody runs out of willpower at some stage. True, some people appear to be more resolute and self-disciplined than others, but understanding willpower and how to foster it is of benefit to everyone.

The information you find here is firmly based on research findings, mainly from the field of psychology and the brain sciences. The information is meant to be applied in a practical way tailored to your particular wishes and needs.

This book is also fun – it reflects my strong belief that enhancing your willpower isn't always hard work and doesn't always involve self-denial. Willpower isn't an internalised police officer telling you what you should or shouldn't do. Willpower is about enabling you to choose your goals and attain them in order to deliver well-being and happiness in the long term. Sure, your willpower needs to say 'No!' or 'Stop!' from time to time, but this is just to ensure that you remain on the path that *you* chose in the first place. If there's more than a hint of a law enforcement officer here, it's one that you've chosen to employ.

Less, therefore, about developing an iron will, more about being compassionate to yourself and learning from your mistakes. In fact, research findings suggest that the pursuit of true happiness (including episodes of spontaneity and self-indulgence!) can promote and sustain willpower. *Excessive* self-control, driven perhaps by perfectionism, can deplete willpower in the long run, or fear of failure can prevent you from even considering changes in the first place.

And one more thing: the Internet and its many multimedia facets has forever changed the world we live in. It provides valuable resources to promote your willpower, both in terms of knowledge and information but also technology. The feedback, reminders and nudges you can get from your smartphone, tablet or other device 24/7 can be an awesome ally when your willpower is flagging, distracted or disengaged. (I designate Chapter 14 entirely to the use of web-based technologies.)

Foolish Assumptions

While I was writing this book, I made a few assumptions about you. For example, I assumed that you've tried and sometimes, or even often, failed to sustain willpower in pursuit of your goals. I think you'll agree that this ensures a potentially large readership!

I also assume that you want to improve your willpower in order to accomplish goals you value. I'm fairly sure that when you picked up this book it wasn't because you agonised over whether to wear your blue suit or your black suit or what toothpaste to choose. On the contrary, I assume that you picked up this book because you've struggled to control your impulses and desires or to mobilise your efforts to start or finish an important piece of work when all you want to do is watch television.

Another assumption is that you've reflected on your willpower-related successes and failures and that you're open to re-evaluating and learning from them.

One assumption I don't make is that you're familiar with the latest developments in what is termed *willpower science*. In the past couple of decades or so researchers have uncovered stunning insights and compelling evidence that reveals the secrets of willpower and how to use them to transform your life. These form the basis of the book.

Icons Used in This Book

Icons are handy little graphic images that point out particularly important information about willpower and how to engage it. Throughout this book, you find the following icons, conveniently located along the left margins:

This icon draws your attention to useful examples – some from real life, some simply to illustrate a point.

This icon directs you to tips and shortcuts you can follow to make the most of your willpower.

Remember the important points of information that follow this icon. When you're faced with challenges to your willpower, recalling these may make all the difference.

 Danger! Ignore the advice next to this icon at your peril!

Beyond the Book

In addition to the material in the print or ebook you're reading right now, this product also comes with some access-anywhere extras on the web. You can find an online cheat sheet containing essential tips and pointers at `www.dummies.com/cheatsheet/willpower`, plus an extra Part of Tens chapter at `www.dummies.com/extras/willpower`.

Where to Go from Here

If you're particularly interested in a topic indicated in the chapter headings or index, just dive in. I wrote the chapters so that you can read and absorb them on their own or as part of the book as a whole.

You may, of course, start at the beginning of this book and work your way through to the end. A wealth of information and practical advice awaits you. Simply turn the page and you're on your way!

Regardless of how you find your way around this book, I'm sure you'll enjoy the journey.

Part I
Getting Started with Willpower

For Dummies can help you get started with lots of subjects. Visit www.dummies.com to learn more and do more with *For Dummies*.

In this part . . .

- Get to grips with the nature of willpower – what it is and how it works.
- Take the first steps in your willpower training programme.
- Make willpower work for you by understanding your personality and your emotions.

Chapter 1

All About Willpower

● ●

In This Chapter

▶ Introducing willpower

▶ Understanding the basics

▶ Looking at willpower as a shared resource

▶ Failing at willpower – addiction

▶ Training your willpower

● ●

*W*illpower is unique to humans. Although all living creatures display purposeful behaviour, only humans have the capability to keep a valued goal alive for years, decades or a lifetime. But choosing to pursue valued goals in the medium to long term is often at the cost of suppressing more urgent desires. Setting your mind on losing weight and getting fit, for example, means you have to rein in the impulse to eat what you want when you want. Managing this double act – maintaining a long-term goal in the face of the lure of immediate gratification or distraction – is what your willpower is designed to do. Your capacity to develop and sustain willpower goes a long way to defining you as a person and determining the quality of the life you live.

Equating Willpower and Success

How often have you thought, 'I wish I had more willpower'? You're not alone. You can't achieve anything without willpower. Willpower is what gets you out of bed at 6 a.m. on a cold morning, makes you scrape the ice off the windscreen and go to work. Willpower empowers you to strive for long-term goals and enables you to resist temptation, regardless of the appetite aroused. But sometimes willpower seems to evaporate, often when you need it most.

Three reasons why willpower is essential for success and happiness are:

- ✓ Willpower enables you to achieve long-term goals and fulfil aspirations.

- ✓ Willpower is essential in order to overcome compulsive habits such as smoking or excessive drinking.

- ✓ Willpower gives you the strength to say no to temptation.

When people are asked to list their strengths or qualities, they usually rate their willpower or self-control the lowest. Lacking willpower is the most common reason Americans give when they fail to make more healthy food choices or just to eat less food.

It seems as if willpower ebbs and flows, and it sometimes seems to evaporate just when you need it most. But remember, for every time you eat too much, drink too much, or party too much, there's likely to be another occasion when you control your appetite or say no to a party invite because you need to make an early start the next day.

The aim of this book is to equip you with the skills to boost your willpower and thereby enable you to fulfil your potential and enjoy good health and well-being.

Strengthening your willpower isn't about restricting the joy or pleasure you get from life, it's about giving you the power to shape your life according to your values and virtues.

Recognising that You Do Have Willpower

Like other skills or aptitudes, how much willpower people have varies from person to person. Your willpower is most likely due to a combination of your genetic makeup and factors such as the type of upbringing, parenting and schooling you had. Regardless of whether you demonstrate high levels of willpower or low levels of willpower, however, you can increase your willpower with practice. Although people who seem to have willpower in abundance can always improve their levels, the majority who struggle most to exercise willpower – perhaps you, because you chose to buy this book – have the potential to benefit even more from guided practice.

It's helpful to view your willpower from a number of perspectives:

✔ As a mental muscle that can be strengthened with practice, but that can also become depleted or exhausted. Just as a rest can reinvigorate you when facing an energy-sapping task, putting your willpower in standby mode enables you to summon more willpower after a break. This can be particularly apparent when using willpower to overcome unhealthy habits or addictions to cigarettes, drugs, alcohol, gambling or food.

In the same way that you rely on a common source of energy whether you're running, cycling or swimming, willpower is a common or shared source of mental energy. Willpower is necessary to control everything you do, think and feel. This means that you need to be careful how you invest your limited supply of willpower. For example, using willpower to control anger because your boss made a sarcastic comment about your work means you're more likely to give in to your craving for chocolate during a break.

✔ As a limited resource that may, on occasion, be unable to cope with the various demands placed on it.

✔ As a skill you can acquire through training and practice. Willpower relies on core skills involving the enhancement of motivation as well as the selection and pursuit of personally relevant goals.

✔ As a necessary but not always sufficient ingredient in maintaining your desired outcomes in the long term. You need to build and nurture your personal, social and cultural assets (such as friends, family, job satisfaction and recreational activities) to create a context within which willpower can flourish.

✔ As a reflection of your goals and values. Focusing on and clarifying your motives and values is vital for harnessing your precious supply of willpower. When willpower wavers, as will surely happen, re-evoking your motives and values can help you go the extra mile.

Willpower isn't an ingredient you're given a fixed measure of, with the lucky (or possibly slightly smug!) among us gifted with a large portion, and the rest of us left struggling to meet our deadlines or reduce our calorific intake in the face of relentless distraction and temptation. On the contrary, willpower is a resource that can be nurtured and developed with practice.

That said, although willpower is undoubtedly necessary to initiate and maintain change in the face of inertia or resistance, it isn't always sufficient. A key theme in the book is that any task that requires willpower is going to be difficult, and you need to be prepared for setbacks.

Understanding How Willpower Works

It seems as if everybody knows what willpower is, or at least what it does. But does anybody really understand how it works? In the next sections I explain what willpower is and why it sometimes seems to vanish when you need it most. The aspects of willpower most emphasised in this book are self-control, self-regulation and self-discipline. Defining willpower is the foundation for the most important part of the book, on how to improve your willpower.

Considering the origins and workings of willpower

'Willpower' is a relatively new term, dating back to the 1870s according to some dictionaries. Somewhat obviously, it's simply an amalgamation of the words 'will' and 'power'.

Your brain evolved into a complex system in order to regulate your bodily functions and your behaviour. For the most part, bodily functions run automatically. You don't have to think in order to breathe – for very good reasons! Breathing requires no willpower.

However, when it comes to behaviour where you have a choice – say between having lunch now or finishing a piece of work – a competition takes place in the brain. Powerful impulses, usually linked to appetites, are pitted against a resourceful and clever regulator. The impulses are often termed *bottom-up processes*, and the regulating willpower is labelled a *top-down process*. The top-down processes are capable of reining in the bottom-up impulses, which is the core dynamic of willpower.

Willpower is usually called on when conflict occurs or a choice or decision has to be made. The context is often one involving strong motives or desires.

In any given situation, it's a case of 'I will' or 'I won't,' or perhaps 'I will now rather than later.' Applied to thoughts, feelings and actions, this capacity for self-control defines our humanity and distinguishes us from other animals.

Some people liken the contest for control of behaviour to a horse and a rider. The horse represents your impulses – the desire for more immediate rewards. If the rider is tired, distracted or unsure of the destination, the horse is more likely to do what it wants (which is also what you want but have chosen willpower to override). The rider, representing self-control or willpower, shouldn't be underestimated, however, and can mostly control the horse. In order to do this, riders need to know their own strengths and weaknesses and also understand the needs and motives of the horse.

Throughout this book, some chapters implicitly address the 'rider' and some the 'horse' – the two systems of your brain that determine the effectiveness of your willpower. Chapter 2, for example, focuses on the top-down or rider skills you use to keep the horse under control. Chapter 4 emphasises the need for riders to have a clear destination or goal, and Chapter 5 reminds riders that they need to be in the saddle for a long time. Chapter 6, by way of contrast, is more about horse sense! Sometimes it may be too difficult to rein in the horse (perhaps it sees another horse it finds attractive, or wants to canter through a green meadow). In this case, the rider may need to choose a different path in advance, or have some treats to hand to distract and satiate the horse. Other chapters are more about the welfare of both horse and rider. Both should be fed a nourishing diet and should avoid stress, keep fit and sleep well.

Researching willpower

Three strands of evidence support the new science of willpower:

✔ Numerous experimental studies support the *willpower depletion* or *ego depletion* model. Roy Baumeister and his team at Florida State University showed that willpower dwindles with use. Researchers assigned groups of people to either willpower-demanding conditions or willpower-free conditions. On arriving at the lab after a period of fasting to ensure that they were hungry, people were ushered into a waiting area suffused with the aroma of freshly baked cookies. In one group, people were required to exercise their willpower and resist the temptation to eat any cookies or other treats like chocolate. They were told that, instead, they could eat any of the radishes that were also on the table.

All participants were then moved to another room where they were asked to complete geometric puzzles as part of an intelligence test. The experimenters were interested in how long each group would persevere in trying to solve the puzzles that were, in reality, insoluble (another ruse employed by researchers in the name of science!). The cookie eaters persevered for 20 minutes, but the apparently willpower-depleted radish eaters stayed focused for just 8 minutes.

A variation of this experiment found that people who were asked to either suppress or magnify their emotional response to a heart-wrenching movie ran out of willpower faster than those instructed to react as they normally would to an evocative scene.

These findings are important because they appear to show that willpower can be depleted in quite diverse ways. The other side of the coin, and one of the inspirations for this book, is that willpower can also be boosted using widely varied techniques and lifestyle changes.

✔ A related series of studies required people to practise small acts of self-control or self-discipline, such as systematically monitoring and improving body posture. People who trained their willpower subsequently fared better when taking on bigger challenges such as quitting smoking.

When scientists used imaging techniques to see what happens in the brains of people when they are using their willpower, they discovered that particular parts of the very front of the brain called the dorsolateral prefrontal cortex (the DLPFC; approximately where your temple is, at the side of your forehead) and the inferior frontal gyrus (a ridge of brain tissue behind your eyebrow, or above your eye socket) work in tandem with sections towards the rear of the brain called the posterior parietal cortex. This is the core of the willpower circuit. By practising willpower with a given task, you strengthen these connections because, as a famous brain scientist said, 'What fires together wires together.' When you subsequently encounter another task requiring willpower, the circuits are more hardwired together and you need to make less effort.

But if you overload your brain's willpower circuit or don't allow it sufficient downtime, it becomes less efficient and your willpower diminishes. (Consider how your legs feel as you climb one, two, three, four or more flights of stairs!) This is why those who had to resist the temptation to eat delicious cookies or who had to over-regulate their emotions ran out of willpower more quickly than their less challenged counterparts. These results are found in the short term only. Researchers predicted that with sufficient practice, the harder working, treat-deprived group would eventually develop more robust willpower, meaning the gain would be worth the pain. This resolves the apparent contradiction stemming from findings that willpower can be both wasted and boosted by practice: you need to traverse the willpower circuit many times, with small improvements in performance on each occasion.

✔ Researchers discovered that changing your mind can change your brain. When current smokers were asked to imagine the long-term consequences of smoking, frontal regions of the brain, including parts of the willpower circuit such as the DLPFC, were activated, and the smokers experienced less craving – compared, that is, with when they were asked to focus on the immediate consequences of smoking, when parts of the brain such as the ventral striatum and amygdala, involved in impulsivity and reward processing, were activated. (See Chapter 6 to discover how to use the 'now versus later' strategy associated with this research.)

A related set of findings show that encouraging people to commit to long-term goals, termed *pre-commitment,* such as putting your savings in an account that requires a month's notice before you can withdraw anything, or not carrying a credit card when you go out shopping, activates a different area of the front of the brain – the lateral fronto-polar cortex. (See Chapter 12 for more examples of pre-commitment.) This area is located approximately behind the middle of your forehead, where the two halves of your brain come together. Engaging different parts of your brain can give your willpower circuit some respite or free some willpower for a more pressing use.

Realising that willpower is a shared resource

Willpower relies on a common pool of mental energy. As well as regulating your unconscious, involuntary functions such as breathing, your brain regulates:

- ✔ **Actions:** Your brain takes part in physical activity, such as when you get out of bed in the morning and eat food.

- ✔ **Emotions:** Your brain helps manage stress and anger, for example.

- ✔ **Thoughts:** Clearly, thinking involves your brain, which keeps your attention on the task at hand and doesn't allow it to wander (usually!).

The really positive thing about willpower is that if you train your willpower in one area, such as by doing physical exercise every day, your willpower becomes more effective in other areas, perhaps in overcoming those chocolate cravings. Using the physical fitness analogy, you expect a transfer of fitness across diverse activities such as swimming, cycling and running, even if you practise only one of these on a daily basis. The same holds true for willpower. If you boost your willpower in one area – say you avoid putting sugar in your tea or coffee – your willpower fitness or capacity is empowered in other areas, such as when you try to stick to that diet or quit cigarettes. This training takes time, though, so don't expect improved willpower overnight!

Training your willpower by practising small acts of self-control works directly by strengthening your brain circuits and control of attention (see the 'Researching willpower' sidebar), but also indirectly by changing your beliefs about your willpower. Self-belief is, after all, central to willpower, so the thought that 'I can find more willpower when I really need it' can sustain you when the going gets really tough.

Training also helps you to recognise your limits. The message to remember is 'Don't overload your willpower.' Instead, aim to gradually increase your willpower, recognising your limits along the way. Even when you've started to train your willpower and you're feeling more confident about your level of resolve, you can still, all too easily, overlook that willpower can be a limited resource, as in the following scenarios:

- ✔ Controlling your intake of high-calorie foods by adhering to a strict diet risks making you less able to subsequently refuse a cigarette or a glass of wine.

- ✔ Maintaining a tactful silence or feigning agreement while listening to your boss expound his philosophy on life makes it more likely that you'll be impatient with other drivers on the way home or more irritable with your partner when you arrive.

- ✔ Spending an hour sorting a niggling but non-urgent problem on your PC makes it less likely that you'll complete the work you logged on to do in the first place. The effort and time spent tinkering with your PC reduces your potential willpower available for the primary task. With regard to willpower, your brain doesn't distinguish between troubleshooting your PC and, say, updating your CV to apply for a new job: both tasks rely on a common supply of willpower. This means that you should tackle the important task first.

In all three cases, the suggestion is that willpower relies on a shared resource. You don't have a separate supply labelled 'willpower for keeping my mouth shut' or 'willpower for resisting cigarettes or chocolates'. But surely, you may think, deploying your willpower on more than one front is a frequent challenge. I agree, but I'm eager to emphasise the limits of willpower from the outset. This is the most important message in the book.

The more positive viewpoint is that, precisely because willpower relies on a common resource or skill set, the benefits of practising self-control with activity A should transfer to activity B. For example, if you plan to quit smoking, foregoing sugar in your tea or coffee for two weeks can increase your capacity to remain smoke-free. Similarly, practising other small acts of self-discipline, such as maintaining good posture at your desk, appears to increase your competence to achieve more daunting goals such as dietary control.

If you're dieting, sticking to your diet is obviously important. But not all the time. For instance, if you're at a long meeting where you're required to keep concentrating and make difficult decisions, and lunch is some hours away, do take the biscuit that's on offer. Resisting the snack, perhaps repeatedly, as the tray of temptation revolves around the table, will deplete your willpower. This may not have any really negative consequences. But consider how important is it to keep focused during a long meeting – a task that requires willpower. Investing willpower in refusing a snack may impair your concentration or lead you to agree to something against your better judgement. Acknowledging the limits of your willpower resource is essential.

Realising that willpower is a limited resource

Think of the last time you did or said something you really wanted to avoid doing or saying (or perhaps when you failed to do or say something you should have done or said). Try to recollect what was happening before this. Were you involved in an activity that required willpower or a big mental effort over an extended spell? Were you tired, frustrated or hungry? If so, your impulsive words or actions most likely resulted from you placing too many demands on your willpower. Because willpower is a limited resource, competition goes on in your brain, and you can't always choose the winner. You can, however, gain some valuable insights from this or similar occurrences and undertake to manage things differently in the future. For example, you can sequence events differently so that, for instance, you're more tactful and controlled at that important meeting, and if you end up shouting and swearing, you do while sorting out your PC!

But this book not only tells you about your limitations – usually, you should be able to stick to your diet and perform at work! The upside of the common resource idea of willpower is the exciting bit. Training or practising one type of willpower – for instance sitting up straight or exercising regularly – spills over to other areas. Put simply, you can train your willpower in the same way that athletes can train their bodies. While a typical athlete's training programmes reflect special aspects of the sport – tennis players don't usually run marathons, and distance runners don't spend hours hitting balls – all work towards what I term *core fitness:* endurance, stamina and general strength. Applied to willpower, this means that practising self-control in one area – for instance, avoiding social networking sites during the working day – generalises or transfers to other areas as your willpower strengthens.

Willpower is not the same thing as tough mindedness, the capacity to be resolute and determined but not necessarily sensitive. True, maintaining resolve and determination are important components of willpower. The key message in this book, however, is that kindness and optimism – especially in relation to yourself – create the context for using willpower to achieve goals and sustain change in the long term. Perhaps even more importantly, tough mindedness is a personality trait that is difficult, or perhaps impossible, to change. Willpower, on the other hand, reflects a series of related skills or capabilities that you can develop and optimise. That's the aim of the book.

Being Aware of Addiction Issues

Addiction can be defined as the compulsive, repeated use of a drug, or the repetition of a behaviour such as gambling or gaming, despite harm or negative consequences to yourself or others.

Addiction is the opposite, or perhaps the frequent absence of, willpower. Overcoming an addiction is probably the biggest challenge to your willpower.

Nobody is entirely immune to addiction in one form or another. Indeed, it may well be that your own experience of addiction prompted you to read this book.

In the past 40 years, 45 million Americans have successfully quit smoking (while still alive!). The majority of these made several or even many attempts before ultimately succeeding. The message is never to be discouraged by initial failure or setbacks; you just demonstrated one more way of how *not* to quit, and will eventually discover how to nail the habit.

Willpower is crucial at all the stages of overcoming addiction, from the initial 'I *will* quit' to the subsequent 'I *will not* resume my habit.' This is the essence of how willpower operates: selecting a goal, taking steps to achieve the goal, and sticking to the goal in the face of distractions and temptations. Although much willpower is needed to make that decision and take those initial steps to change, during the ensuing weeks, months and years willpower is truly tested. That is why Chapters 7, 8 and 9 focus on maintaining change, and Chapters 10 and 11 offer guidance on how changing your outlook and your lifestyle can help you sustain change.

Concurrent and/or intensive use of drugs renders your willpower ineffective. You may need specialist help to overcome an addiction, especially to substances such as alcohol, cocaine or heroin. You may find this book helpful, but it's not a substitute for treatment. If you or somebody close to you is concerned about your drug use, seek an opinion from a suitably trained healthcare professional or counsellor.

Increasing Your Willpower

Can you really learn to improve your willpower? In a word, *yes!* Only in recent years have psychologists demonstrated that you can actually train your willpower in the same way that an athlete trains every day before the big event.

Smokers aiming to quit turn out to be more successful at quitting if they practise small acts of willpower or self-discipline in advance of their quit day. The willpower-training tasks, such as squeezing a handgrip up to and beyond the point of mild discomfort, or remembering to maintain good posture rather than slouching, bear no obvious relationship to the trials and tribulations of quitting smoking. Nonetheless, those who practise these small acts of self-discipline prove more robust when faced with the challenge of putting their smoking days behind them.

Identify something you do every day, perhaps by habit, that you can change. This doesn't need to be a big challenge to willpower; in fact it should be something easy to do. Examples of things you can try to do are:

- Sitting up straight at your desk.

- Avoiding swearing or bad language. (Apologies if this would *never* apply to you!)

- Doing a small domestic task such as making your bed every morning, emptying the dishwasher or tidying your desk.

- Using the stairs instead of the lift or escalator (within reason, and taking account of any health concerns).

- Choosing a healthy option at lunch – the low-fat version – or choosing an Americano rather than a cappuccino during your coffee break.

- Not eating standing in the kitchen; prepare your food and then sit down and eat.

- Skipping the visit to your favourite social networking site during your coffee break.

- Questioning your beliefs about willpower. If you run out of willpower and think, 'I knew I didn't have much willpower,' try and recall examples when you *did* sustain your willpower. Developing a more balanced or positive belief about your willpower may empower you next time you're wavering.

Resisting marshmallows

In the 1960s and early 1970s, Walter Mischel and his colleagues at Stanford University carried out a series of experiments testing young children's self-control. The *marshmallow experiments,* as the studies came to be known, entailed leading children aged between four and six into an especially fitted-out room in the psychology department. The room was free from distractions, apart, that is, from a series of treats including marshmallows, pretzels and cookies placed on a table. The children were told that they could eat a marshmallow immediately or wait 15 minutes and have two.

More than 600 children completed this test of the ability to resist temptation. Many children, particularly younger ones, immediately grabbed the marshmallow, but about a third were able to defer gratification for the required period and were duly rewarded with two marshmallows.

These children relied on a number of strategies, including imagining that the marshmallow was a fluffy cloud, tugging at their pigtails or even kicking the table leg (perhaps it was the little boys who did this!).

This was just the start of a study that continued for several decades, with many of the participants followed up as they grew into adults. Those who showed more willpower as youngsters, by not immediately eating the marshmallow, were subsequently found to do significantly better at school and college. As adults, they appeared to enjoy more satisfying and rewarding relationships and have lower body mass index, all of which suggest that they continued to overcome the impulse to eat the marshmallow! Factors such as IQ didn't account for this greater success, so it wasn't simply that those who could command more willpower were more intelligent.

Congratulations! You just started your willpower training programme! In the same way that a long-distance runner first practises over a shorter training course, or a weightlifter begins at the lower end of the range, acquiring the willpower habit begins modestly. Beginning with one or more of these small steps helps you succeed with larger goals.

In some scenarios, on some days, you seem to have the knack of imposing your will; in other situations, on other days, you're left bereft of the focus and power of your will. As I explain in later chapters, this fluctuation isn't random: you can anticipate when your willpower is likely to be challenged and take steps to prevent succumbing to temptation.

No book can claim to provide the secret of perpetual willpower, and this isn't my purpose here. What I can provide are the tools you need to harness the extraordinary power of the will to help you achieve your goals and improve your well-being. You can maximise your willpower!

Chapter 2

Willpower and You

*Y*our willpower emerges in infancy. The child who can resist the temptation to eat sweets is more likely than others to mature into a self-disciplined adult. You may think that a tendency first expressed in childhood that then endures into adulthood is a reflection of personality and cannot easily be changed. If that was true, however, there would be no point in me writing this book, or indeed in you reading it, because personality doesn't normally change throughout the lifespan.

Willpower is more than a personality characteristic: it's also a mental strength or talent. It's partly innate, but it can be cultivated and grown. Your personality influences the strength of your willpower but doesn't determine it.

Willpower can, however, be directly influenced by emotions such as fear, anger, sadness and joy. Understanding your personality and being more aware of your emotions can help you use your willpower effectively and help you understand why it sometimes fails.

Linking Personality and Willpower

Understanding your personality can help you make your willpower work for you. Recognising and accepting that you're spontaneous and impulsive, for example, can help you anticipate when your willpower may be challenged. You can use your willpower to bypass going on a shopping spree, in order to save for an adventurous holiday. You thereby nurture your quest for excitement or stimulation in a way that's ultimately more enriching than yet another trip to the shops.

 Maximising your willpower is about improving your well-being – not about becoming a predictable and dreary robot! It's less about self-denial, more about choosing when and where you can have fulfilling, pleasurable and enriching experiences.

Exploring the Big Five Facets of Personality

Five dimensions, or relatively independent factors, define your personality and everyone else's. Most people are in the middle zone rather than at the extremes, but the personalities at the far ends help define those in the middle. The Big Five can be combined to form the acronym OCEAN (or CANOE if you prefer!):

- ✔ **Openness:** This refers to being open to new experiences. If you tend to seek out novel or diverse experiences, and you find routines dull and boring, you're likely to be strong on this personality attribute. You may also be creative and independent, but occasionally impulsive.

  Openness, like any of the Big Five, isn't necessarily the best personality trait in all situations. If you're high on this dimension, you may find yourself easily distracted. This can weaken willpower in some situations where a narrow, more down-to-earth approach is better. Following a complex recipe in the kitchen, for example, requires you to focus on the ingredients and quantities and on completing the steps in the right sequence. You can always be imaginative in your choice of wine!

✓ **Conscientiousness:** If you're strong on this dimension, you're likely to be dependable, self-disciplined and achievement-orientated. You may be rather less spontaneous and find it unsettling if a plan is changed or comes undone. If you're not strong on this dimension, you may be rather carefree and impulsive.

✓ **Extraversion:** This is one of the better-known personality characteristics. Extraverts are sociable, assertive and outgoing. At the other end of the scale, introverts can be reserved and comfortable being alone.

✓ **Agreeableness:** This personality characteristic reflects the degree to which someone is friendly and compassionate versus being more critical, tough-minded or unkind. Clearly, a disagreeable disposition can be problematic within a family or in the workplace, but being overly agreeable – saying yes when you should politely say no – can cause problems in due course.

✓ **Neuroticism:** I prefer to call this emotional sensitivity, because the adjective neurotic appears judgemental. Regardless of the term used, your own and others' emotional responsiveness is clearly a definitive aspect of individuality and personality. If you frequently experience feelings of sadness, anxiety or anger, perhaps on a daily basis, this probably reflects the influence of this personality characteristic. At the other extreme, lacking emotional sensitivity means that you may not be able to empathise with others or experience the full palette of emotions that enrich human experience.

No ideal personality profile exists for delivering a constant supply of willpower, but extremes on any dimension can cause problems.

Rate your personality according to the five facets in Table 2-1. Respond spontaneously without agonising over your choice – remember that no right and wrong answers exist! Everyone has these personality traits; they're not labels or categories. Circle the number you feel best represents your personality on the scale.

Table 2-1	Mapping Personality						
Openness	I'm focused and prefer convention and routine.	1	2	3	4	5	I prefer novelty, creative or intellectual stuff and stimulating environments.
Conscientiousness	I'm spontaneous, fun-loving and carefree.	1	2	3	4	5	I'm usually well-organised, dependable and achievement-orientated.
Extraversion	I'm quiet and reserved, and I can be quite happy on my own.	1	2	3	4	5	I'm sociable, outgoing and talkative.
Agreeableness	I don't suffer fools gladly, and I can be argumentative and irritable.	1	2	3	4	5	I'm good-natured and compassionate.
Emotional sensitivity	I'm a calm person and usually in control of my emotions.	1	2	3	4	5	I tend to worry a lot, and I get upset easily.

This isn't a formal, validated psychological test. If you type 'Big Five personality factors' into your search engine, you can find a wealth of information on the Internet, or you can visit http://personality-testing.info/tests/BIG5.php to answer 50 questions and obtain a more detailed Big Five personality profile.

What's your personality like? If, for example, you scored high on extraversion and openness but low on conscientiousness, you may have more difficulties in exercising willpower than someone with the opposite characteristics. You probably enjoy life to the full and are seen by friends as fun-loving, spontaneous and game for a laugh. But consider a scenario in which you spontaneously opt to go partying instead of choosing to study or have an early night before a long day at work. In this case you may need a rethink, guided by an understanding of your personal preferences and priorities.

Table 2-2 shows how rankings on each of the Big Five facets of personality can influence willpower.

Table 2-2	Personality Traits and Willpower	
Personality Factor	*Risk to Willpower When High*	*Benefit to Willpower When High*
Openness	Easily distracted; become bored by diet or health routines	Creativity; good problem-solving skills
Conscientiousness	Perfectionistic; self-critical following setbacks	Self-disciplined, purposeful, goal-orientated
Extraversion	Impulsive; high sensitivity to instant rewards (hedonistic)	High level of social support; capacity to discover new rewarding pursuits
Agreeableness	Lack of assertion; being a 'people pleaser' can tax willpower when pursuing personal goals	High level of social support; self-compassion when willpower fails
Emotional sensitivity	Negative emotions sap willpower and motivation	Emotional awareness; overcoming negative emotions offers big incentive to change

It's easier to build on your personality strengths rather than waste willpower overcoming perceived weaknesses. For example, if you're an extravert, you're probably better off working in sales or the hospitality industry rather than as a librarian cataloguing books. Lifestyle choices that are aligned with your personality can promote your willpower by enabling you to be more confident and competent.

Being predisposed

The term *disposition* and the concept of being predisposed to doing something is derived from astrology: the idea is linked to the *position* of planets or stars at the time of birth. This illustrates that the quest to understand ourselves and our motivation has long preoccupied humankind, although the position of the planets and stars has no known influence on willpower, personality or behaviour.

Willpower isn't an independent personality factor but can be influenced by different patterns of the Big Five. Conscientiousness, for instance, which reflects self-discipline and motivation, appears to capture the essence of willpower. Surely conscientious people will always get the most from their willpower? Well, yes, until they encounter a setback. In that event, the fact that things don't go according to plan causes more difficulty than with a less conscientious individual. Conscientiousness can merge into perfectionism. Similarly, being too agreeable can jeopardise your capacity to exercise willpower, if you keep saying 'yes' when asked to do somebody a favour.

You're not a prisoner of your personality! Personality reflects a tendency to act in a particular way in certain situations. You can use willpower to influence how you behave. For example, you can decide to overcome your shyness and talk to a stranger at a party; likewise, you can keep the party animal in you at bay when you have to finish a work project.

Reading Your Feelings

Emotions are a vital component in our common evolutionary legacy and key to our survival. Understanding and correctly labelling your emotions is crucial for effectively conserving and using your willpower.

Emotions such as anger, fear or sadness can soak up your willpower by dominating the more reflective systems of your brain that support willpower. In Chapter 1, I use the analogy of the horse and rider to illustrate that while the horse, representing your emotions and impulses, is much stronger, the rider, representing the rational self, is usually in control. But if the rider's willpower is distracted, the large, powerful horse may seize the opportunity and bolt.

Think of a time when you were angry or upset. Did you do, eat or drink something without any conscious intent or recall? This is an example of how willpower can be neutralised by emotions. When evoked, strong emotions can override (I'm thinking horse again!) your planned actions. All well and good if that keeps you out of the way of a speeding lorry that ignored the stop signal; using your willpower here to decide to carry on crossing the road in order not to be late for work could land you in hospital – or worse!

The five primary emotions are:

- ✔ Fear
- ✔ Anger
- ✔ Sadness
- ✔ Disgust
- ✔ Happiness/joy

Your emotional experience undoubtedly is multi-layered and complex, incorporating a range or combination of emotions at any given point, but ultimately all your emotions draw from the core emotions in this list. Shame, for example, may incorporate fear of criticism or punishment combined with disgust directed at your own transgression.

Emotions can exert their own overwhelming willpower when triggered. This effect can literally be life-saving or life-preserving, for example if you jump out of the way of a speeding vehicle, or instantly feel revulsion for food that's unfit to eat. In this context, emotions are gifted with a licence to temporarily command and control your behaviour.

Emotion is in the eye of the beholder

Your emotional response is always authentic, but it can be based on a misperceived or distorted view of the situation. For example, you may be fearful about a forthcoming public-speaking event or a job interview, because you overestimate the probability that you won't be offered the job, assume that not receiving a job offer would be truly awful, and underestimate your ability to cope with the anticipated rejection and misery. Without doubt your emotional experience feels real, but it's based on faulty assumptions.

Jumping to conclusions or making assumptions that prove to be untrue can cause emotional false alarms. This can disrupt your willpower in two ways:

- ✔ Emotions simply impose their own fundamental willpower in the moment and override the goals you're pursuing.

- ✔ Repeated emotional false alarms can lead to lasting emotional distress that can drain your limited supply of willpower.

Keying in on the truth

Rushing to work one day, I slammed the door behind me and then noticed that my keys weren't in my pocket. I thought, 'How stupid. I must have left my keys in my other jacket.' I immediately felt my irritation physically. I then heard a welcome and familiar tinkling noise from my bag: my keys were in the front pocket of my briefcase! I immediately calmed down and continued my journey to work.

In this case, my emotions weren't influenced by the exact location of my keys, but by where I believed they were. My emotional response – a mixture of anxiety about being able to get into my home later on that day and frustration at my own apparent stupidity – was authentic but based on a fallacy.

This illustrates how the key (no pun intended!) to managing your powerful primary emotions is realising that your thoughts are just thoughts and not necessarily true. Epictetus, a philosopher in Ancient Greece, put it like this: 'People are not disturbed by things, but by the view they take of them.'

In the here and now, biased or incorrect patterns of thought can be more subtle, such as when you predict that you may not perform well at a job interview, or assume that an invitation to a party isn't genuine. These negative views can make you feel anxious, unhappy or avoidant, even though they're just thoughts and may be wrong. Just like my belief about my keys.

Negative emotions are more compelling

You may have noticed that in the list of primary emotions at the beginning of this section, negative emotional states outnumber the sole positive emotion of happiness. Negative emotions such as fear and anger are a key part of our evolutionary legacy because of the survival advantage they confer. If our evolutionary ancestors hadn't had these powerful reflexes, we wouldn't be around today!

Bear in mind, however, that while negative emotions are intense and impossible to ignore, they're often short-lived.

Connecting Your Emotions and Willpower

Emotions are neither positive nor negative, but clusters of mental, physical and behavioural responses that help you survive and adapt. So-called negative emotions are like an SOS signal: highly specific but inflexible. Negative emotions are, nonetheless, commanding and have the power to override your willpower. Emotions such as fear and anger enable you to survive in the heat of the moment, and fuel your response to a dangerous situation, whether that entails flight or fight.

Given the pressures of modern living, the emotion of fear, which is designed to save you from sudden threat or danger, can be too readily evoked and can cause distress. Think of fear as an emotional false alarm.

Imagine being overwhelmed by feelings of anxiety or self-consciousness during a job interview. These emotions may be prompted by unhelpful and largely untrue beliefs that you're likely to embarrass yourself and perhaps be ridiculed as a result. Regardless, you may feel a strong impulse to leave the situation, and you may well find yourself heading for the nearest exit.

This example of emotionally driven behaviour illustrates the way in which powerful emotions can override your willpower. That's why understanding and managing your emotions effectively is crucial to maximising your willpower.

Negative emotions deplete your willpower. If you're feeling frustrated, angry or tense in relation to a task that requires willpower, follow these steps:

1. **Focus on your feelings and take note of them.**

   For example, say to yourself, 'I feel angry because I have to do this' or 'This is making me feel anxious.'

2. **Manage your emotions:**

   • Take a short, active break doing something that switches your attention away from the negative emotion. This may be leaving your desk and going outside, ideally to woods or a park, and paying attention to what you see.

   If you can't leave your desk or home, or you're already outdoors, try doing something different, such as making a phone call instead of trying to compose an email. Or practise mindful breathing or mindful walking.

   • Review the thoughts or beliefs associated with the negative feelings. You may find that you've been paying too much attention to the negative aspects of a situation and discounting some of the positives.

Appreciating the Role of Positive Emotions

Hopefully, you find yourself most often in a normal emotional state – in the zone of contentment, fulfilment, happiness or joy. This cluster of positive emotions is a product of evolutionary pressures that enables us to think creatively, solve problems, form intense and loving relationships and build lasting social networks. Being happy isn't just a good thing in itself, it's also a context for promoting willpower.

Positive emotions such as joy or happiness have less urgency but more creativity than negative emotions. When you feel fear, you only have to select between fleeing or fighting, but happiness – or the pursuit of happiness – creates a rich array of options. Table 2-3 shows the predominant thoughts and actions associated with positive and negative emotions.

Table 2-3	Thoughts and Behaviours Associated with Emotions	
	Negative Emotions	**Positive Emotions**
Thoughts	Simple, clear, immediate. For example, 'I must run' or 'I hate him'	Elaborate, speculative, exploratory. For example, 'I wonder whether next week will be as interesting as this week' or 'I'm really enjoying the party. It's a shame I have to leave in an hour'
Behaviour/ Actions	Flee, avoid, escape, attack	Approach, engage with others, explore, savour the moment

Log on to www.moodpanda.com, a free-to-join web resource than allows you to monitor your mood. You can also download apps for iPhone or Android smartphones. Monitoring your feelings helps you identify when your willpower may be reduced by stress or when it's a good time to take on a willpower challenge.

Considering Your Beliefs about Willpower

If you've struggled to exercise willpower, you may have thought, 'Self-discipline! I don't have much' (or any). Reflect for a moment on your first impressions when you read words such as 'willpower' or 'self-discipline'.

In this section, I give you hints so that you can develop a more balanced understanding of yourself and your willpower. Your beliefs about willpower, regardless of how accurate or representative they are, can become self-fulfilling prophecies. If you believe that you have little or no willpower, you may not stick at a task that's easily within your grasp. By not attaining goals – in effect, by quitting too soon – you come to believe more and more that you're lacking willpower. It's less a self-fulfilling prophecy, more a vicious circle.

Consider this scenario: identical twins Sharon and Suzy decide to go on a diet. Despite their identical appearance and shared upbringing, the twins think differently, especially about themselves and their willpower. Nonetheless they choose a diet, agree on a start date, an exercise regime and (identical!) weight-loss goals. Five weeks into the new regime, the twins have mixed results, both having lost weight initially and then regained some but not all of it. Table 2-4 shows how the twins' thought patterns diverged.

Table 2-4   The Twins' Beliefs about Willpower

Suzy's Thoughts about Willpower	Sharon's Thoughts about Willpower
I've never had very much willpower.	Sometimes I've used willpower effectively; on other occasions less effectively.
If I don't lose weight, it's because I don't have enough willpower.	If I don't lose weight, it's because I didn't choose a good time to diet.
This is typical: I get things right for a while and then I fail. I'm almost back where I started.	This is proving a bit more difficult than I thought! I can learn lessons from this. I lost 3 kilograms, gained 2 back, so I'm still ahead of the curve!
This has left me feeling exhausted; I want to quit this diet!	This is taking a lot of effort, but at least I'm trying. Practice makes perfect!
It's my fault that I haven't succeeded. *And* it's my boss's fault for putting me in charge of a challenging project.	Overall, my limited success with this diet is due to a number of factors: timing, planning and work pressure.
If I can't get this right, I can't get anything right.	Sticking to a strict diet isn't one of my strengths, but I do have strengths!

Suzy displays the style of thinking that can make her feel bad about herself and reduce her ability to benefit from the experience and apply any lessons learned to improving subsequent efforts. First and foremost, Suzy asserts that she's always lacked willpower. In contrast, Sharon appreciates that willpower can vary. Suzy also has a tendency jump to conclusions ('If I can't get this right, I can't get anything right'), to over-generalise ('This is typical . . . I'm almost back where I started') and to fall into the blaming trap ('It's my fault . . . It's my boss's fault').

I can now reveal that Suzy and Sharon are the same person! This illustrates that different beliefs and assumptions about will-power can influence how you may react to setbacks. Looking six months ahead, which style of thinking – the Suzy mode or the Sharon mode – do you think will deliver a better outcome? Without doubt, Sharon's flexible thinking style makes her more resilient and protects her from the negative feelings that deplete willpower. If Suzy was a real person, I'd recommend that she reads Chapter 7, as indeed should you if you think like she does!

Part II
Taking Seven Steps to Improved Willpower

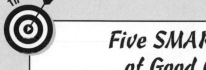

Five SMART Ingredients of Good Goal Setting

A good goal should be

- ✔ **Specific:** Write your goal simply and clearly define what you're going to do.

- ✔ **Measurable:** Make your goal measurable. You need to be able to tell when you've reached your goal or how close you are to achieving it.

- ✔ **Attainable:** Ensure that the goal you set is actually achievable. Be honest with yourself and ask whether you have the capability – the knowledge and skills – to achieve the goal.

- ✔ **Realistic:** Ask yourself how feasible or realistic your goal is. For example, you may have the motivation and ability to train for a marathon, but if you're about to change job or become a parent, training intensively may not be such a good idea!

- ✔ **Timely:** Embed your goal within a clear timeframe. More a case of 'I'll put my name down for the pottery for beginners class that starts next October' than 'I'd love to do something creative like learning pottery'.

For some great online extras about willpower, head online and visit www.dummies.com/extras/willpower.

In this part . . .

✔ Gather the tools you need to focus, strengthen and increase your willpower.

✔ Prioritise your goals to make the most of your willpower.

✔ Use willpower to give you the stamina to sustain change in your life.

✔ Stay alert for the triggers that drive your habits and challenge your willpower, and find out how to cope with them.

✔ Avoid the negative feelings that sap your willpower and reduce your motivation to learn from setbacks – and reset your goals.

✔ Mobilise your behaviour and maintain your motivation in pursuit of long-term goals.

✔ Employ your memory to help you stay focused on your goals.

Chapter 3

Training Your Willpower: The Willpower Workshop

*M*ost of the time, you can safely rely on your willpower: you can drag yourself out of bed in the morning even when you're tired, politely refuse a second helping at the dinner table, or switch off the television to complete a work project. But sometimes your willpower appears to vanish, and you do precisely what you said you wouldn't do – or indeed fail to do what you promised to do. Yes, willpower comes and willpower goes. In this chapter, I explain how to maximise your willpower. This is achieved in much the same way as athletes or musicians prepare for a big event: by recognising the challenges they face, having the right plan and the right diet, and practising with the right exercises.

Willpower is a scarce resource, so you need to spend it wisely! Developing and using the willpower toolkit helps you do this. The toolkit is divided into four sections: problem solving, diet (especially ingredients for a healthy brain), physical exercise and mental exercise.

Developing Problem-Solving Skills

Just like your ancestors who discovered tools to help themselves survive, you need to learn what tools to choose, when to use them and when they are best left in the toolkit. It makes sense, then, that the first section of this chapter focuses on problem-solving skills. The key word here is *skills*. You, like everyone else on the planet, encounter problems each day. You often solve them intuitively, without having to exert too much effort or indeed use too much willpower. But you need to approach some problems – the kind that require sustained effort or willpower – carefully, with a plan of action. That's the best way to focus your willpower.

Distinguishing between worrying and problem solving

To develop problem-solving skills, you need to recognise the difference between worrying and problem solving. Doing so is easier said than done, because you can easily assume that worrying helps you solve a problem. It doesn't. Worrying gives you the illusion of control or the sense that you can anticipate and therefore prepare for difficulties in the future.

Consider something that you worried about in the past. (This shouldn't be difficult, because everybody worries, and 38 per cent of people worry every day.) The worry could be focused on your health, your personal relationships, your performance review at work or whether your car will break down on a long journey. Next, recall an occasion when something difficult, unwanted or untoward did in fact occur. This can, of course, be from the preceding list, but can you honestly say that what you worried about was an accurate prediction and prepared you for the problem? Obviously, if you draw up an exhaustive list of everything that can possibly go wrong, the likelihood is that, among the list, you'll hit on the one thing that will go belly up. The focus of your worries is limited only by your imagination! The downside to this is that you'll have exhausted your supply of willpower by ruminating on all the unwelcome scenarios that didn't occur. Worrying wastes willpower.

On the other hand, a *problem* is something with a *solution* –
a series of steps that you can take to prevent, resolve or mitigate an unwanted or unwelcome event or outcome. Thus,
you can worry, to no good effect, about the possibility of
rain ruining your barbecue or picnic, but hiring a marquee
(or arranging for your guests to be issued with umbrellas!)
directly addresses the problem.

Table 3-1 highlights the differences between worrying and
problem solving.

Table 3-1   Differences between Worrying about a Problem and Solving a Problem

	Worrying	*Problem-solving*
Thought Process	Repetitive, rumina-tive. For example: 'I hate my job; I'm not performing well.'	Defines the problem and identifies steps to take to address it.
Typical Behaviour	Passive, restless or avoidant.	Active, purposeful and engaging.
Emotional Impact	Anxious, restless, pent-up energy.	Your energy is chan-nelled into action.
Typical Coping Style	Emotion-focused. For example, avoidance or substance use to get rid of negative feelings.	Problem-focused. For example, willpower used to implement a plan. This gets to the root cause of the emotion (i.e. the problem), meaning that you may have to tolerate distress initially but the likeli-hood of recurrence is reduced.
Effect on Willpower and Motivation	Depletes willpower and motivation.	Utilises willpower (and thus depletes it), but can boost motivation.

Worrying about a problem won't solve it; in fact, worrying
wastes precious mental energy and saps your willpower. As
Lady Macbeth put it: 'Things without all remedy should be

without regard. What's done is done.' This means that we're better off learning to accept some things, such as ageing, ill-health, disability or the loss of a valued role, even if this is difficult or painful. Recognising the sometimes inevitable losses prevents you wasting your willpower. This is important, because you need all your willpower to deal with the consequences of any loss. If you've lost your job, for example, worrying about the future, although understandable, doesn't help you get another job. Problem solving does.

Inevitably, you're prone to worry when confronted by ill-health or the realisation that you're not getting any younger. Dwelling on your lost youth is not necessarily helpful, and possibly depletes your willpower. On the other hand, aspects of ageing such as being unfit, gaining weight or losing ambition are problems that can be defined and addressed. This is problem solving in action.

You know you're worrying if you're having the same thought over and over again (for example, 'I must change my job because I don't get on with my boss'). In contrast, problem solving is about planning and doing (for example, thinking, 'I'll update my CV and register with an employment agency'). Practising problem solving is the most effective way of spending your willpower.

The key to successful problem solving, and to using your willpower efficiently, is to learn acceptance in the face of the inevitable, but creativity in response to the solvable!

Using the 5W1H approach

The five Ws, one H (5W1H) approach is a useful tool to help define a problem and suggest potential solutions. The five Ws and one H represent questions you ask about a problem you're trying to solve. Ask yourself:

- ✔ What is the problem?
- ✔ Who is affected; who is it about?
- ✔ Why is it happening?
- ✔ Where is it happening?
- ✔ When is it happening?
- ✔ How can I solve this problem?

List as many options as you can think of then choose one or two for variety.

After answering the questions, take steps to achieve your goal.

This approach to defining and addressing problems originates in the writings of the ancient Greeks. In mediaeval times, similar questions were put to sinners in order to ensure their confession covered every facet of the sin!

Whatever the problem that assails you – being overweight, struggling to get out of debt or feeling stuck in a relationship in which you're not loved or valued – techniques such as 5W1H help you to get the measure of the problem, understand your motivation to solve it and begin exploring potential solutions. Granted, problems are not always easily solved. But with willpower on your side and the right approach to problem solving, you can lose weight, control your spending and manage your relationships better.

Audrey wants to lose weight and uses problem solving, based on the 5W1H approach:

✔ **What** is the problem?

 Audrey is not as physically fit as she used to be.

✔ **Who** is affected; who is it about?

 Because her goal is a personal one, the answer to Audrey's question is herself or, more specifically, her willpower. At this stage, Audrey can identify a friend, family member or colleague who can be supportive in her quest to improve her fitness.

✔ **Why** is it happening?

 She values physical and mental fitness.

✔ **Where** is it happening?

 At work; some days Audrey has to travel across several sites. She stopped playing tennis, because her tennis partner had more stamina than she did.

✔ **When** is it happening?

 In the mornings, Audrey worries about the day ahead and her limited stamina. In the evenings, after work, she sometimes feels exhausted.

✔ **How** do I solve this problem?

At this stage, Audrey explores possible solutions to the problem:

- Walk to work three days a week

- Walk home from work two days a week

- Cycle to and from work

- Get off the bus/train a stop earlier on her way to work or home

- Take up a sport

- Join a gym

- Buy a running machine/exercise bike for home or the workplace

- Go swimming three times a week

- Take up jogging

- Get a dog!

Audrey decides to get a dog and take it running!

You may have to address some additional issues on the way to achieving your goals. For example, if you want to lose weight and choose jogging as one of the answers to the 'how?' question (I'm speaking from experience here, because I recently took up jogging!), you have to ask yourself a few more questions:

✔ Are you medically fit? If you have a history of cardiovascular disease or problems with mobility, check with your doctor first.

✔ Do you have the right clothing and footwear? If not, the first step is to go shopping for these.

✔ Do you have a route in mind?

Just do it! If your problem is simple, for example your car is due for a service or the pipes in your bathroom are leaking, you don't need to work out a problem-solving plan! Just type 'car maintenance' or 'plumber' in your search engine, hit return and make that call. As a rule, your best plan with straightforward problems with obvious solutions that require no more than five or ten minutes is to address them promptly and get them done. This helps preserve your quota of willpower for bigger challenges, and also reinforces your self-image as a doer rather than a delayer!

Feeding Your Brain: The Willpower Diet

The first step in preparing to train your willpower is to do some basic brain maintenance to ensure that your brain is healthy. Like any bodily organ, the brain requires nutrition to do its job and stay healthy. Brain cells, in common with other cells in the human body, can be damaged by rogue atoms or molecules known as *free radicals*. Fatty acids are important for maintaining healthy brain cells and good connections between them.

If your brain could choose food from the menu, it would make sure the dishes contained a plentiful supply of glucose derived from foods that release it slowly, such as nuts, vegetables and legumes such as beans and lentils. For maintaining a healthy brain, fatty acids such as omega-3s and antioxidants including vitamin E and vitamin C should also be on the menu.

Preventing your brain from getting rusty!

A popular theory links ageing, especially that of the skin, to the effects of free radicals. These potentially toxic chemicals come from a variety of sources including environmental pollution, cigarette smoking and exposure to the sun, and are produced by the body's own metabolic processes. A free radical is unstable and needs to bond with molecules in other cells, but in the process can disrupt the functioning of its new-found host. An analogy for this is rusting, an example of oxidation.

Brain cells are especially vulnerable to oxidative damage linked to free radicals, so foods such as spinach, broccoli and potatoes, which contain antioxidants, are the ones to go for. Vitamin E, found in vegetable oils, green leafy vegetable and nuts is another good antioxidant. Vitamin C can be found in citrus fruits and vegetables. By eating these foods, you are, in effect, rust-proofing your brain!

Avoid sugary foods such as sweets and fizzy drinks. True, these can increase your blood sugar levels, and this can temporarily boost your willpower. That is precisely why willpower researchers use glucose drinks in the laboratory. In the lab, the rapid change in glucose levels is important to clearly demonstrate its relationship with willpower. But a sudden increase in glucose levels also triggers the release of insulin to reduce the spike in blood sugar, so outside the lab the benefits may be minimal and/or short lived.

Fatty acids, such as omega-3s, and antioxidants are important to maintain the smooth and efficient operation of the brain. They act a bit like the lubricants and cleaning agents in an engine. But glucose (blood sugar) is more like fuel. The harder you work your brain, especially in tasks requiring willpower, the more glucose you need.

Avoiding a diet that reduces your willpower

In the USA, obesity rates have increased by 75 per cent over the past 30 years or so, and more than one-third of the population can now be classified as obese. This unwelcome trend has been observed in most developed countries, and approximately a quarter of UK adults can now be classified as obese.

Obesity can be defined in different ways, though you're usually regarded as being obese if you're 20 per cent above your normal or expected bodyweight. *Body mass index* (BMI) gives a more precise measure of whether you're overweight (see the 'Calculating your BMI' sidebar).

No doubt there are many reasons for the sharp increase in obesity: higher disposable income, longer working hours, cheap fast food, to name but a few. The obesity epidemic appears to be linked to significant changes in diet, with a shift towards processed foods that are high in sugars and saturated fats so as to be more palatable and moreish. At the personal level, however, this reflects a challenge to willpower.

Individuals rarely choose to be overweight; on the contrary, people strive very hard to lose weight. Clearly, quitting smoking or other drugs is difficult, but surely a change of diet should be less of a challenge to willpower.

Evidence now suggests that what's known as the *Western diet* – one high in saturated fats and high-glycaemic-index foods such

Calculating your BMI

You can calculate your body mass index (BMI) using the following formula:

Your weight (kilograms) ÷ your height (metres squared)

The formula captures the necessary link between height and weight. You can calculate your BMI on the websites of the National Heart, Lung and Blood Institute, and the National Health Service (at `www.nhlbi.nih.gov/` `guidelines/obesity/` `BMI/bmicalc.htm` and `www.` `nhs.uk/Tools/Pages/` `Healthyweightcalculator.` `aspx?Tag`).

A BMI in the range 25 to 30 is regarded as evidence of being over-weight, and individuals in the 30 to 40 range are classified as obese. Normal BMI is in the low 20s, and scores of 18 or 19 suggests that you may be underweight.

as sugar – can affect your working memory, the vital component of willpower that's essential for keeping your goal uppermost in your mind. Without this memory, you tend to forget your goal and your willpower loses its focus. Studies of human and animal subjects confirm that the Western diet impairs learning and memory by disrupting brain maintenance.

For the technically minded, high levels of fat and glucose disrupt *neurotrophins,* substances produced in the brain that protect cells in the hippocampus, a pivotal part of the brain's memory circuits.

The effects on working memory may be very subtle, but any reduction in your brain's efficiency can reduce your willpower. Consider this as a circular process where the behaviour you want to change – eating a high-fat, high-sugar diet – takes the edge off the memory and willpower tools you need to accomplish the job.

If you're trying to lose weight, before you eat recall what you ate for your last meal, whether it was breakfast, lunch or a snack. People who do this eat less at the current sitting. This also requires relatively little willpower, leaving you better able to resist the temptation to order a sinful pudding!

Realising that the quick fix is not the best fix

The quickest way to fuel your brain with glucose is to eat or drink something sugary. But this is not the best way, especially if one of the reasons you choose this book was to control your diet! You need foods that release sugar slowly, so your glucose levels fall slowly over a longer period. This is a bit like filling your tank with fuel that might not give you rapid acceleration but will get you farther!

Researchers tend to give glucose to the participants in their studies precisely because it triggers relatively quick increases in blood glucose levels followed by quick decreases. This makes it ideal in the lab, where time is of the essence. Drinks or foods high in glucose aren't recommended in the real world, because rapid fluctuations in glucose levels are not good for either your metabolism or your brain.

Avoid buying processed foods whenever possible. Anything that comes in the guise of a sauce or a packaged meal is likely to be loaded with extra salt and sugar. Even basics such as tinned beans are usually drenched in a sauce charged with flavour enhancers like salt and sugar (would you normally put sugar on your beans?). Eating out should entail careful choices: butter has been termed the chef's secret weapon, and pizzas contain high levels of salt.

Foods can be classified according to the rate at which your body metabolises their carbohydrates into glucose (sugar). That's not the full story, however. Some foods (a cream cake, for example) deliver a rapid uplift in glucose after eating, followed by a rapid decrease. Other foods release glucose more slowly. Examples include most beans (white, black, kidney and so on), small seeds (sunflower, pumpkin, sesame and the like), most common vegetables, and sweet fruits (including cherries, strawberries and peaches).

Foods that release their energy more slowly – those that food scientists call *low-glycaemic-index foods* – are generally the best choice for breakfast and lunch on a working day. (Take a look at *The GL Diet For Dummies* by Nigel Denby and Sue Baic (Wiley) for more information about low-glycaemic foods and stacks of tasty recipes.)

Beat the brain drain

A team of researchers from universities in Florida and Texas recruited 103 undergraduates and divided them into two groups. They measured their blood glucose levels and asked each group to watch a six-minute video that required either high or low levels of concentration.

The group that had to concentrate hard – calling on more willpower – showed significant reductions in blood glucose level. They subsequently showed impaired performance on another demanding task. However, when they were given a glucose drink, this group's performance recovered.

This is one of several studies to show that your brain uses glucose more quickly when working hard – striving for goals or overcoming habits. This helps explain why you can feel exhausted from purely mental effort, because of course glucose is a source of energy not just for the brain, but for your entire body.

Matching food to willpower challenges

What's the best diet to enhance your willpower? Generally, sustaining glucose levels for longer rather than shorter periods is crucial to maintaining willpower, so you want to eat foods low on the glycaemic index. If, for example, you're striving to remain a non-smoker, you need the endurance of a marathon runner more than the power of a sprinter.

Willpower enables you to control the choices you make, and high-glycaemic foods can sometimes be the right choice. If you're feeling exhausted at the end of a long working day and dinner is two hours away, a bar of chocolate can sustain you (if your goal is to quit chocolate, ignore the last sentence!). If you're approaching the end of a long drive, a pit stop for coffee and something sweet may be the right choice. A boost of glucose may help sustain your willpower for the last leg of the journey, and reduce the likelihood of you getting a speeding ticket because of poor control over your speed – an example of willpower failure.

Maintaining willpower increases the energy demands on your brain. Glucose, a product of carbohydrates, is your brain's favourite energy source. By carefully choosing foods that release glucose over relatively shorter or longer periods – typically ranging from 15 to 20 minutes to perhaps 1 to 2 hours – you give your brain what it needs to take on and win the willpower challenge!

Nature's delicious secret is dark chocolate containing more than 70 per cent cocoa. This has remarkable health-giving properties. It's rich in antioxidants, omega-3s and important vitamins and minerals such as potassium and magnesium. It also contains phenylethylamine, the same chemical your brain releases when you fall in love! Like other types of chocolate, dark chocolate contains fats and some caffeine, so don't overdo it. You can, however, use dark chocolate, perhaps a small amount each day, as a way of rewarding yourself, or just as pure self-indulgence!

Taking Physical Exercise

Brain scientists have now confirmed what many suspected for years: staying physically fit is not just good for your physical health, it's also good for your mental and emotional health. When you move your muscles and limbs on purpose, your brain becomes more active.

Put simply, it appears that both brain cells and the connections between them respond positively to physical activity, especially *aerobic* activity that stimulates the heart and respiratory system. An active brain with healthy cells and a good communication system is more likely to deal with the challenges of using willpower.

Australian researchers Megan Oaten and Ken Cheng measured the benefits of exercise by following a group of students who exercised regularly and comparing them with those who didn't exercise regularly. They discovered that after just two months of exercising between one and three times a week, the regular exercisers showed significant decreases in:

✔ Perceived stress

✔ Emotional distress

✔ Smoking

✔ Alcohol and caffeine consumption

✔ Procrastination or delaying decisions

The participants who exercised regularly also showed significant increases in:

- ✔ Healthy eating
- ✔ Emotional control
- ✔ Maintenance of household chores
- ✔ Attendance to commitments
- ✔ Monitoring of spending
- ✔ Improvement in study habits

Laboratory tests indicate that these changes were associated with improved attention and the ability to ignore distractions – the key components of willpower.

What I find striking about the list is that many of the changes are precisely those that people strive for only to find their willpower lacking. It appears that regular exercise is one of the quickest ways to improve willpower.

So how much exercise does your brain need to boost your willpower and well-being? The answer is that any regular exercise such as brisk walking is likely to produce benefits, although about three hours a week for 20 to 30 minutes a day is advisable. What are you waiting for? Go do it!

By setting yourself a goal of daily or near-daily exercise, you're actually taking the first step in training your willpower, as well as preparing your brain for more difficult willpower challenges ahead.

Be specific about taking steps to achieve your goal. Instead of the more general statement, 'I'll exercise for a while a few times a week,' try a tailor-made plan: 'When I come home from work on Monday, Wednesday and Friday, I'll jog down to the river and back home through the park.'

Being specific takes a bit more effort and planning to begin with, but reduces the effort subsequently required to put your plan into action. Research shows that people who develop specific plans are more likely to achieve their goal and less likely to be distracted.

Exercising Your Brain

Your brain is always active and never sleeps. When you're firmly in idle mode – sitting on a train or staring blankly at the television – your brain is busy monitoring the world around you and regulating your bodily functions. Brain scientists call this the *default network*. This network is activated when you're not focused on a particular task, and is involved in daydreaming and mind wandering, as well as maintaining vigilance and keeping you prepared for action. Even when you're gently (or maybe loudly!) snoring the night away, your brain is busy, particularly when you're dreaming.

So why does your brain need to be exercised if it's always on the go? The answer is that while your brain is generally active, even when you're resting or sleeping, the circuits involved in generating willpower can be powered down. (If you've not looked at Chapter 1 yet, see where a sidebar describes the particular parts of your brain that are involved in the focused, sustained effort that characterises willpower.) You need to exercise this more particular 'willpower circuit'.

The serious point is that mental exercise aimed at improving specific brain functions, such as keeping a goal in mind and overcoming distraction, is more effective if it involves variety, challenge and novelty. Just as in the section on physical exercise I recommend brisk walking as the minimum required for brain-beneficial activity, mental exercise needs to stretch or challenge you in order to be effective.

Whatever occupies your working memory, usually in the form of a goal or objective, influences what you pay attention to. In order to keep one goal in mind – catching that train, rescheduling the dentist's appointment or remembering to log on and pay an outstanding bill – you need to keep other information out, because working memory has limited capacity. Maintaining a healthy and well-exercised brain helps you to meet this challenge.

 Training your brain can be fun and can also involve doing meaningful and valuable work. Apart from formal training packages available online or on a smartphone, a wide range of activities and pursuits can give your brain a workout. Developing a new hobby, learning to play a musical instrument or mastering a new language meet the criteria of variety, challenge and novelty important for optimising your brain power and thus increasing your willpower. Likewise, getting involved with local community organisations or political causes exercises your brain. All these activities require your brain to process information, which is your brain's preferred and only form of exercise.

After you've decided what activity you want to practise to enhance your willpower, tell a friend or loved one (this could be one and the same person!) what you propose to do. Not only does this increase the potential for support, but the act of sharing information helps you remember your goal!

Developing Your Willpower Muscle

A balanced diet, regular physical exercise and mental stimulation all contribute directly to your capacity to maximise your willpower. Without doubt, striving to maintain a healthy brain itself requires willpower. Please don't be discouraged if, having read this chapter, you've concluded that your diet is poor, you avoid physical exercise and relax by watching reality television! I wrote this book with you in mind. So before making any changes to your lifestyle or habits, try one of the following exercises, which are known to boost your self-control skills.

Identify something you do every day, perhaps by habit, that you can change. This doesn't need to be a big challenge to your willpower; in fact it should be something relatively easy to do. For example, you could aim to:

- Sit up straight at your desk.

- Avoid swearing or bad language (apologies if this would *never* apply to you!).

- Do a small domestic task – making your bed every morning, emptying the dishwasher or tidying your desk.

- Use the stairs instead of the lift or escalator (within reason, and taking account of any health concerns).

- Choose a healthy option at lunch – the low-fat version – or choose an Americano rather than a cappuccino during your coffee break.

- Skip the visit to your favourite social networking site during your coffee break.

When you've chosen something from the list or determined your own habit to break, you've embark on your own willpower-training programme. Congratulations!

If you're about to set yourself a new goal or challenge, such as getting fit or quitting a bad habit like smoking, practising small acts of self-control for a week or so can boost your chances of success. You can practise and improve the core skills of willpower – keeping a goal in mind and avoiding distraction – in the same way that a long-distance runner first practises over a shorter training course or a weightlifter begins at the lower end of the range. Acquiring the willpower habit should begin modestly.

Chapter 4

Zeroing in on a Single Goal

● ●

In This Chapter

▶ Understanding your working memory

▶ Identifying your values

▶ Choosing SMART goals

▶ Nudging your willpower

● ●

*T*he biggest threat to willpower is the innocent-sounding and well intentioned to-do list. A to-do list is okay, as long as it has only one item in it! Choosing goals such as increasing your productivity at work, losing weight, quitting smoking and spending more time with your family are unquestionably worthy objectives. However, should you attempt these in *parallel* rather than in *sequence* in your quest for a brand-new you, you're likely to achieve little or perhaps just short-term success. Your willpower is a limited resource and will quickly become overstretched if you try to make many changes at once.

Prioritising one goal doesn't mean abandoning your ambitions in other areas. It does mean that you tackle it first and remain single-minded in pursuing it.

The good news is that your *working memory,* your ability to store and process information moment by moment, is adept at maintaining your chosen goal. It just needs motivation to ignite the effort and willpower to maintain it. Working memory is the best ally your willpower has. Getting to know your working memory and appreciating its strengths and limitations helps you remain single-minded and successful.

Affirming your values helps you choose your first goal – your priority. This ensures that you're using your willpower to achieve something personally meaningful. Appreciating your values and determining what motivates you also enables you to avoid wasting willpower in pursuing goals that may seem desirable but are not aligned with your values.

Working Memory: Your Brain's Desktop

When working on your PC with documents and files, it's usually helpful to save them temporarily to your computer's desktop. Parked there, the files remain visible, accessible and easy to update. For example, the draft of this chapter is on my desktop, but when it's finished I'll place it in its long-term home, a folder named, unsurprisingly, willpower.

The human brain has evolved a very specialised function, known as working memory, that operates somewhat like your PC's desktop folder. *Working memory* enables you to store and manipulate information for short periods – measured in seconds and minutes rather than hours and days.

Contrasting working memory and long-term memory

Using your working memory effectively is the key to harnessing your willpower, because willpower lapses happen in moments, not months. In contrast to long-term memory, which enables you to store information and knowledge about yourself and the world right back as far as your childhood, working memory focuses on the present and the immediate future.

When I'm introduced to somebody new, I can usually remember the person's name for a few minutes, as long as it remains in my working memory. But if I meet the same person a couple of hours later, it's often a case of, 'I'm sorry, but I seem to have forgotten your name!' However, if I rehearse the name by repeating it to myself, I can subsequently recall it with ease. This is because I've transferred the name into long-term memory, from where I can quickly retrieve it into working memory.

Rehearsing your goals makes them easier to retrieve and install in your working memory. This is crucial, because if you fail to maintain your goal in working memory, your willpower is of no use to you. Willpower can fail simply because you forget what you're aiming to do. The distraction may be only momentary, but finding ways to keep your goal in mind and avoid pesky distractions is vital to maintaining willpower.

Being single-minded

Your working memory has limited capacity, which is both its greatest strength and its greatest weakness. Try composing a text and maintaining a conversation at the same time – you can't do it if either or both tasks are at all complicated.

Even though texting requires dexterity (or texterity!) of the hand, and conversation requires listening and speaking, both tasks require your working memory to process information. Unfortunately, your working memory is single-minded to a fault. When fully loaded, it's obliged to prioritise, so it's either text or talk!

You can use the limited capacity of working memory to aid your willpower by ensuring the goal you choose is given pride of place. That helps prevent competing goals, distractions and temptations gaining access to your working memory, and shows that sometimes a limitation can prove to be an asset.

Imagine a conflict between competing goals. One goal is to get up 30 minutes early to meditate, the other goal is to get 30 minutes' more sleep. Your working memory can only fully accommodate one goal at a time. If this is the 'meditate for 30 minutes' goal, the 'sleep 30 minutes more' goal fades away (and of course the converse is only too true!). The goal awarded pride of place in working memory influences your subsequent flow of thoughts, as shown in Table 4-1.

Table 4-1	Justifying Competing Goals	
	Goal: Get 30 Minutes' More Sleep	*Goal: Meditate for 30 Minutes*
Thoughts Supporting the Goal	It's warm and cosy; sleep is as good for me as meditation; that was a wonderful dream.	Meditation prepares me for whatever happens during the day; meditation is good for my brain.
Object of Focus	Comfort of warm bed, soft pillow, insulated from reality.	Stillness of early morning; calmness of mind that follows meditation.
Likely Behaviour	Stay in bed.	Get up and meditate.

Think of the competition for space in your working memory as a horse race with only one prize. First past the post gets the prize – the ability to direct subsequent thoughts and actions. It's a case of winner takes all. Actively rehearsing and recalling your goal, so it becomes more familiar, is the best way to give it a head start in the horse race.

Putting working memory to work

Late one night, I was driving on the motorway and noticed I was very low on fuel. The next service area was 25 miles further on, so I exited in the hope of finding a local filling station. As my low fuel warning light continued to flash, I slowed instinctively several times when approaching distinctive yellow, red or green neon signs, only to discover myself slowing down for restaurants, pubs and hotels.

Consciously, I knew the neon was unlikely to point to a source of fuel, but nonetheless my attention was grabbed by the signs, and I experienced an impulse to slow down. The goal of getting fuel was in my working memory and guided my attention towards cues that might help me achieve my goal.

In this scenario, working memory was helpful, because it was surely better to be vigilant rather than miss the target – which, fortunately, was just around the corner!

Looking at Motivation: The Essence of Willpower

Whether in pursuit of a valuable goal or in the quest to suppress an unwanted habit, defining and focusing on your motives provides a good launch pad for your willpower. It seems safe to assume, for instance, that if you're reading this book, you were motivated at least once, otherwise you wouldn't have it in your hands!

Motivation mobilises your behaviour in pursuit of your goals. Without motivation, willpower becomes irrelevant – it doesn't matter what you do or don't do or how much effort you invest.

If improving or maintaining your health isn't a motive, you don't bother to watch your calorie count or consider quitting smoking. If achievement or success aren't motives, failing an exam or losing your job is irrelevant.

Choosing the right goal at the right time

Goals are the single most important motivator of behaviour. Identifying and striving for goals provides meaning and structure to your life. Without goals, people become inactive and even depressed.

Selecting a personal goal doesn't require much willpower, but achieving it does.

Think of your willpower as a personal asset that you can invest in pursuit of a range of goals. Like any shrewd investor, you want to invest wisely. But this investment isn't about financial gain – although it could be, depending on your goal – it's about remaining true to your values. Choosing goals aligned with your values ensures that you're motivated to strive for successful attainment. I offer options to help you identify, or perhaps to rediscover, your values in the upcoming section 'Identifying Your Values'.

Identifying priorities: Your personal balance sheet

The message of this chapter is that being single-minded and focusing on one primary goal at a time is the best way to utilise your willpower to maximum effect. This means choosing goals carefully and pursuing goals in sequence, one after another, rather than in parallel.

One way to do this is to rate your goals in terms of importance and urgency. For example, it may be important to update your CV, but if you have no plans to change job, it's not urgent. Look at Table 4-2 for examples of urgent and not-so-urgent goals. There's no fixed formula; for example, renewing your passport isn't urgent if you aren't planning to travel abroad, but it's important nonetheless.

Table 4-2	Rating Goals According to Importance and Urgency: An Example	
	More Urgent	**Less Urgent**
More Important	Renew my passport, which is about to expire; quit smoking	Join a health club; eat a healthier diet
Less Important	Buy the latest version of *Tomb Raider*	Wash my car; sell my old CDs

Fill in the blanks in Table 4-3 with your own goals. The goal in the top-left section is where you should focus your willpower!

Table 4-3	Rating My Personal Goals According to Importance and Urgency	
	More Urgent	**Less Urgent**
More Important		
Less Important		

Identifying Your Values

If you find identifying your goals and estimating their importance and urgency difficult, it may be because you're leaving out a key ingredient: your values. Above all, your values define you and distinguish you from others.

Imagine, for example, that you mysteriously lose your values and are, in effect, a moral blank slate – a value-free zone – rather like Oscar Wilde's definition of a cynic: 'someone who knows the price of everything and the value of nothing'. Next, imagine that a minor miracle occurs, and personal value restoration is enabled. Without necessarily prioritising – I don't think values can be rank ordered – my list looks something like this:

- ✔ Honesty
- ✔ Compassion/kindness
- ✔ Loyalty
- ✔ Genuineness
- ✔ Humorousness
- ✔ Modesty
- ✔ Willingness to learn
- ✔ Sharing my knowledge and skills
- ✔ Helpfulness to others
- ✔ Rationality

This is the first time I've tried this exercise, and I'm not claiming that I can always live up to these personal values. I do my best. I was genuinely surprised that the values appear to be a good fit for my personal and working life, consistent with the fact that I'm fortunate to be happy and content for the most part. By way of contrast, if I was in a different profession – a captain of industry or a politician – modesty (or perhaps honesty, with regard to the politician!) might not be such helpful values to have. I might need to add tough-mindedness and perhaps place compassion farther down the list.

You may find gaps between values you aspire to. For example, you may value loyalty, as indeed I do, but occasionally be confronted by conflicting loyalties. You may value the benefits of organic foods, but find you have insufficient time or energy to prepare meals, and opt for convenience foods instead. This simple example illustrates how identifying your values can help you choose goals wisely and invest your willpower in pursuing goals that matter to you.

Compose your own list of values and use it to prioritise your goals.

Knowing what you value steers you away from seductive but ultimately unimportant goals. Your goal may be to seek promotion and greater earnings at work, but if pursuing money doesn't sync with your values, your commitment and resolve will fade sooner rather than later, in effect wasting your willpower. For example, if you value being of service to others, choosing to become a manager of nurses to earn more money rather than staying in a direct patient care role may weaken your motivation and cause you to lose sight of your goal.

Willpower is a scarce resource; use it wisely.

 In pursuing goals, you need to become a *willpower miser* and be very careful about how you spend your precious and limited willpower resource. For instance, you can reduce the number of routine decisions you need to make by shopping for groceries online and reordering each week with a few minor amendments from time to time. Or you can subscribe to automated alerts from your bank to stay on top of your overdraft facility, thus freeing the small amount of willpower needed to log on or phone your bank.

Setting SMART Goals

Knowing your precise goal is vital. Similarly, framing your goals carefully and precisely is crucial to managing your willpower effectively.

Your working memory – your 'getting things done' memory – needs clear goals. A good way to do this is to make your goals SMART. SMART is an acronym representing the crucial ingredients of good goal setting:

> ✔ **Specific:** A goal should be simply written and should clearly define what you're going to do. 'I'm going to lose 2 kilograms each week for a month' rather than 'I'm going to shed some weight.'

✔ **Measurable:** A goal should be measurable. This may sound obvious, but you need to be able to tell when you've reached your goal or how close you are to achieving it. (The example in the Specific point meets this criterion, because the target can be met, exceeded or not achieved.)

Being able to see your progress is important in managing your willpower, because you need to estimate how much more of this precious commodity you may require. Alternatively, if evidence shows that you've reached your goal, you can deploy your willpower elsewhere. You can also reward yourself for interim success, which is the key to motivating sustained effort. (Chapter 7 refers to ways to reward yourself.)

✔ **Attainable:** A goal should be achievable. You need to be honest with yourself by asking whether you have the capability – the knowledge and skills – to achieve the goal. Invariably, attaining a goal requires some effort or challenge on your part, but you need to have confidence that you can actually achieve your purpose if you persevere. For my part, I've concluded that writing this self-help book is achievable, but writing an award-winning literary novel is not! As somebody once said, there's a novel in most people, and that's where it should stay!

If you tend to be a perfectionist, basing your self-worth on being able to achieve mastery in whatever domain you choose, be careful not to over-stretch. Think, 'I'll learn to order meals and book my travel in French,' rather than 'I'll learn to speak French like a native.'

✔ **Realistic:** You need to ask yourself how feasible or realistic your goal is. For example, you may well have the motivation and ability to train for a marathon, but if you're about to change job or become a parent, training intensively may not prove to be such a good idea!

✔ **Timely:** To coin a phrase, 'Tomorrow never comes.' Your goal therefore needs to be embedded in a clear timeframe. More a case of 'I'll put my name down for the pottery for beginners class that starts next October' than 'I'd love to do something creative like learning pottery.' Or 'I'll have two alcohol-free days, beginning next Monday,' rather than 'I'm going to drink less alcohol.'

Consider the following statements:

I want to visit Paris.

I want to fly to Paris for a week in April, after I've received my pay rise.

Although neither of these goals requires much willpower, which do you think is more likely to result in a memorable holiday? While it takes a little more effort to form the SMART goal, defining your objective this way makes it more likely you'll achieve it.

Prioritising, Preparing and Performing

After you've chosen your goal but before you commit any precious willpower to obtaining it, you need to address three key questions, called the Three Ps:

- ✔ **Priority:** How much of a priority or how important is the goal to you?
- ✔ **Preparation:** How prepared or ready are you to pursue it?
- ✔ **Performance:** How confident are you that you can achieve it?

For example, you may see quitting smoking, losing weight or studying more effectively as very much a priority, but not feel prepared to take on the challenge, and lack confidence in your ability to achieve the goal. The big plus point here is that you recognise the need to change but you also acknowledge the obstacles.

You can now focus on preparation and maybe practising the skills that you need to improve your chances of success. (Check out Chapter 3 to see how you can train your willpower for particular challenges.) In contrast, you may be very confident that you can perform effectively to achieve the goal, but if you don't think it's important or you think the timing isn't right, it's best to preserve your willpower for a time when your priorities change or a more opportune moment arrives. If you have a goal in mind, use Table 4-4 to try the Three Ps approach.

Table 4-4	Three Ps: Priority, Preparation, Performance				
Goal:					
	Not At All	*Somewhat*	*Not Sure*	*A Lot*	*Very Much*
Priority: How important is it to me?					
Preparation: Am I ready?					
Performance: Can I deliver?					

If you find yourself ticking the 'Not Sure' or 'Somewhat' boxes, ask yourself why you're not ticking the 'Not At All' box. If you're somewhat prepared and somewhat but not very confident about striving for a particular goal, some reason must explain why you didn't tick the 'Not At All' box. For example, if you're not confident that you can stick to a low-calorie diet, you can remind yourself that you successfully stopped smoking sometime earlier (or vice versa). This may move you towards the right side of the table by clarifying your priorities, improving your preparation and boosting your subsequent performance.

Ways to Nudge Yourself

Nudge theory emerged less than a decade ago. The aim of *nudge theory* is to subtly guide people's decision-making and choices, particularly with regards to behaviour that influences health and well-being. Placing healthier foods such as fruit and vegetables at eye level in the supermarket is an example of nudge theory; banning junk food is not! The aim is to seamlessly influence behaviour using more carrot (or possibly by more carrots!) and less stick. You can use the principles of nudge theory to create a more willpower-friendly environment.

Nudge theory

Do you get spam? Of course you do; everybody gets spam. This is because you probably had to opt out instead of opting in to allow your email address to be used to inform you of the unrepeatable offers that seem to recur nonetheless. You've been nudged! Not ticking the box means that you didn't summon up the tiny amount of willpower necessary – most likely because you didn't read the small print – to opt out.

Nudge theory has more lofty aims as well, and can be used to give willpower a helping hand (or at least elbow!). A school in England placed the salads, fruits and vegetables at the start of the food counter, so the kids selected these first, thus filling their plates with healthier foods. The children ate much more healthily as a result, even though they didn't have to use any willpower. A hospital department informed out-patients that 90 per cent of people turn up on time, and this increased attendance rates further. Perhaps the oddest example of nudge theory in practice is that when a fairly realistic fly was painted on to the urinals at Amsterdam's Schiphol Airport, the floors remained cleaner due to more accurate urinating by the (presumably male!) visitors. None of these examples entail telling folk what to do or not do with signs or warnings – they're more subtle nudges.

Your willpower can become exhausted by you making decisions. If you can arrange your environment to support your goals, then you can conserve willpower. For example, if you're using willpower to exercise regularly, consider packing your training gear the night before and placing it in the hallway where you can simply pick it up as you head off for the day. Or, similar to the supermarket display, place healthy food products more prominently on your shelves and in your fridge, again nudging your choices. This requires planning, which, of course, also uses willpower. But it's all about timing: you can formulate your 'nudge' plans at a time of your choosing when fewer demands are made on your willpower. This is like using electricity at the cheaper off-peak rate!

Consider these examples:

- ✔ When preparing a shopping list, begin by listing the healthiest foods.

- ✔ When planning a meal, start with deciding what vegetable and salads to eat, then match a fish, meat or vegetarian dish to complement this.

✔ If you have difficulty getting up on time or tend to over-sleep in the morning, put your alarm clock out of reach – even in a cupboard.

✔ Book several sessions with your fitness coach so that you have to use willpower to opt out rather than simply show up.

✔ If you have a fitness app or have signed up to an online fitness programme, enable the email alerts to either remind you about exercise goals or provide motivation-enhancing feedback.

Chapter 5

Recognising that Change is a Journey that Takes Time

· ·

· ·

*Y*ou need motivation to embark on change, but you need willpower to sustain it. Often, the decision to change seems a no-brainer: your doctor may tell you that you're overweight, or your boss may tell you that you're not pulling your weight! Seriously, challenging news about health, wealth or performance can act as powerful motivators for change.

But catalysts are short lived, and resolution can quickly turn to dissolution. Willpower becomes more important the farther you travel down the road to change. Motivation provides the energy for the initial sprint, but willpower gives you the stamina to complete the marathon. Recognising the milestones on the journey of change helps you to navigate and orientate, and to optimise your willpower.

Seeing the Cycle of Change

Change is a process, not an event. Psychologists describe change as a cyclical process involving the stages shown in Table 5-1 and explained in the next sections.

Table 5-1	Willpower and the Process of Change		
Stage of Change	*Level of Willpower Required*	*Willpower-enabling Thought*	*Associated Action*
Precon-templation	Zero. Perhaps occasional awareness that some-thing needs to change.	'My partner thinks there's a problem; I don't.'	You become aware of a need to change.
Contemplation	Low to mod-erate. No commitment to imminent action.	'There are some good things but also some less good things about this area of my life.'	You involve loved ones or close friends in your decision.
Preparation	Moderate; occasion-ally high. Commitment to action within days or weeks.	'I've made a decision; now I need to plan and implement it.'	You practise small acts of self-control such as adopt-ing a physi-cal exercise regime and keeping a record of the behaviour you want to change.
Action	High. You're now taking steps to change and are experienc-ing conflict choosing new, less familiar behaviours and suppress-ing familiar behaviour patterns.	'I'm saying no when offered a cigarette; I'm not buying any more cigarettes; I'm not smoking any more.'	Reward your-self for effort, either by saying 'Well done!' or with a treat.

Stage of Change	Level of Willpower Required	Willpower-enabling Thought	Associated Action
Maintenance	Moderate. New behaviour patterns are becoming more practised and require less effort.	Remind yourself of your motives for embarking on change: 'I'm going to evening classes to improve my career prospects; I don't smoke, in order to stay healthy.'	If your change programme means avoiding people or places (friends who continue to smoke, for example) don't isolate yourself. Broaden and build your social networks.
Relapse	High. This is the critical stage in the process of change. Responding to a lapse or relapse determines the outcome of the planned change.	Instead of thinking 'I failed,' consider 'Since January, I've been 95 per cent successful.' Identify *triggers* – the people, places, or things that preceded the lapse.	Put the setback in perspective. If you bought and smoked a pack of cigarettes, count the days, weeks or months you remained smoke-free.

The sixth stage, relapse, is one you don't want to go through, but inevitably will. I talk about that in the upcoming 'Relapse' section and in Chapter 7.

Precontemplation

This can be described as the 'ignorance is bliss' stage of change. If you're precontemplating, you're in denial, whether it's about the hazards of smoking or excessive drinking, or the need to address some problem in your life. (At this point, your denial is slipping, because you're starting to acknowledge that indeed you have a problem!)

If you're concerned that somebody close to you, or perhaps somebody you supervise or manage, may be causing themselves harm by smoking or excessive drug use, confrontation is not the best strategy. Challenging a person's denial can generate resistance and defensiveness and make matters worse. You may then lose your role as a potential influencer. A better way to respond to precontemplation is to tactfully raise awareness, encouraging any talk of change and reinforcing alternative behaviours. Acknowledging the obvious value your affiliate or colleague places in the behaviour can also help. For example, 'You're working very long hours in order to keep on top of things at work, but have you thought that this means you're not getting enough time to relax or get sufficient sleep?' is more likely to start a discussion than an argument.

Contemplation

Ambivalence is the hallmark of this stage of change. If you find yourself musing along the lines 'On the one hand . . . and on the other,' welcome to the contemplation club, where the members sit firmly on the fence! Nonetheless, you're thinking about change, and that moves you closer to taking steps to change.

Preparation

At this stage you progress from thought to action, perhaps testing the waters with tentative changes in your behaviour. For example, you update your CV in preparation for a career change (or simply locate the most recent copy). Preparation is about small steps, orientated towards your goal. These small steps are nonetheless important because they can boost your willpower and self-confidence. This makes it easier for you to identify and pursue the next step, which could be posting your CV online and contacting a recruitment consultant.

Action

This stage is about implementing change: your quit smoking date has dawned; you start an evening class to learn that foreign language; you make your new-year-resolution-fuelled visit to the gym.

As you start developing your new habit to replace the old one, defer difficult decisions or projects, if possible.

The most common outcome at this stage is – you guessed it! – dropping out or quitting. By all accounts, the gym is a less crowded place in March or April that it is in January!

When you fail to accomplish what you set out to do, your negative emotions can compromise your willpower. Fortunately, if this happens early in the change journey, the sense of personal letdown is not as strong as it would be months or years later. If you have a setback, think 'I'll go back to the preparation stage and rethink my plan.'

Maintenance

Having taken action to accomplish a goal, you can throttle back your willpower a bit as you reach cruising altitude. This phase is about consolidating the change you made – in effect, 'stamping in' the new patterns of behaviour.

Refusing a cigarette becomes easier with practice; routinely visiting the gym on the way home from work also requires less effort. I use a very simple exercise to illustrate this when teaching people about habits. I first ask them to write their names as usual, using the dominant hand. I then asked them to transfer the pen to their other (usually left) hand and try again. The result is always an illegible scrawl, following painstaking effort! This is because writing the name with the dominant hand is stamped in, just like any highly practised routine of behaviour. I've never asked my students to practise the new way of writing their signatures until they are stamped in (if I did, I suspect I'd get fewer applicants for my courses!), but if they were to practise they would gradually become partially ambidextrous – an example of stamping in.

If you're fortunate to achieve your goal without too many setbacks, you have a good indication that you'll continue to succeed. Good beginnings lay good foundations for long-term change. Don't forget that you're using willpower, nonetheless. Try not to become complacent, and remain focused on maintaining the change you've successfully initiated.

Reaching for the stars

Chris Hadfield, who was commander of the International Space Station, had a dream. No, it was not to become a YouTube sensation by singing David Bowie's *Space Oddity* ('Ground control to Major Tom . . .') in zero gravity. Hadfield's dream, early on, was to become an astronaut.

Chris's quest to become a spaceman began when he was nine years old. Along with his family, he crowded into a neighbour's house to watch the television broadcast of Neil Armstrong stepping onto the moon on 20 July 1969. Young Chris was captivated. He was also aware of the obstacles. He's Canadian, and Canada didn't have a space programme. Only US citizens could join NASA (the National Aeronautics and Space Administration).

The hurdles to becoming an astronaut didn't deter Chris from joining the Royal Canadian Air Force and training as a fighter pilot. He also studied hard and trained as an aviation engineer. Eventually, the possibility of a secondment to NASA came about. In the face of intense competition from the best pilots in the United States Air Force, Chris was offered a place on the space station training programme.

Hadfield sustained his goal for more than 40 years. This guided his behaviour and choices along the way, and shows willpower at its best. (And, during this time, he also learned to play the guitar!)

Hazardous habits, like smoking or overeating, can take years to develop, and a long, if not necessarily equal, time to overcome. You need your willpower over long spells to override old habits. Be particularly vigilant when you're tired, stressed or hungry, because old habits can break through when your willpower is at a low ebb.

The brain networks that developed to orchestrate your habits don't entirely disappear, they just get overwritten by new brain patterns as new habits emerge. The good news is that as you replace bad old habits with good new habits, your willpower becomes more and more efficient. Habits are easy to start and hard to stop, regardless of whether they're bad for you or good for you.

Relapse

Coping with a relapse – in effect, falling backwards or going back to square one – is the most difficult thing you'll ever ask of your willpower. At the moment when you're feeling most demoralised because you failed at your stated goal, you need to go back to an earlier stage of contemplation or preparation and decide whether to try again.

All is not lost. You've discovered a situation or context that reveals your willpower weakness. You can use the situation to plan ways to avoid the situation in the future. Also, despite the setback, you've undoubtedly strengthened your willpower simply by getting to the maintenance stage of change.

Chapter 7 deals in much more detail with how to cope with a relapse.

Realising when it's Okay to Quit (or Quit Quitting!)

Willpower is a limited and precious resource, and you can't afford to waste it in futile effort. That would be like throwing good money after bad. You should invest your willpower in using viable tactics in pursuit of attainable goals.

Of course, it's hard to determine when your chosen strategy is ineffective or to acknowledge that a goal is proving to be beyond reach. There's a fine line between knowing when to persevere and when to take a step back.

A useful tactic is to decide in advance how much time or effort (corresponding to the amount of willpower) you want to allocate in pursuit of a particular objective. For example, you may decide to limit yourself to making three job applications for a new role. Or you may give yourself three months to lose 10 kilograms of weight.

If you have unrealised objectives, in due course this doesn't mean that you should check your ambition, but you may want to press the reset button. Recall that willpower is necessary but not sufficient to achieve change. Timing and context are crucial, so it may be better to conserve your willpower sometimes.

Willpower is about persisting with effort, not about setting yourself up to fail repeatedly. If change is a journey, you are the navigator, and you decide whether to alter the course or the destination.

Review and reflect

If you're experiencing a dilemma about whether to persevere in the face of a lack of success or negative feedback in relation to your goal, you can review two things:

- ✔ **Your goal:** Consider whether your goal is actually attainable, or attainable at this time. Chapter 4 talks about how to choose a goal.

- ✔ **Your strategy:** Look at the plan you formulated to help you achieve your goal in simple steps. (Chapter 8 offers a guide to making changes step by step.) You can also use online resources to guide the pursuit of your goal (www.goalwriter.com, for example).

After reviewing your goal and strategy, you can decide whether redefining your goal or shifting your tactics justifies the investment of more willpower.

Avoid the grey zone of ambivalence and make a clear decision. The 'will I, won't I?' type of conflict leads to negative rumination and is associated with worry, depression and physical health problems. Worrying depletes your willpower directly because when you're brooding you can't think straight, and perhaps indirectly because of potential mental and physical health problems.

Contemplating change can be a moderate drain on your willpower, so the sooner you decide whether to pause or proceed, the more willpower you can preserve, whether for resuming the original challenge or in pursuit of another goal.

Recall an episode when you chose to disengage from attempts to solve a problem or strive for a goal. My guess is that you felt a sense of relief, hopefully followed by an improved sense of well-being.

You're entitled to choose your goals, and you're equally entitled to disengage from them. Unless there's a degree of urgency related to your health or well-being – quitting smoking or changing your diet, for example – the timing of most personal goals can be flexible.

Don't be shy about sharing your dilemma with trusted friends and loved ones.

No such thing as a short-term diet exists. Granted, you may have every intention to make it last forever, but most diets aimed at reducing weight or promoting health attain historical status! Simply accepting this is the first step in preparing for the challenge of change in the long term.

Good project managers anticipate failure in order to prevent it. Imagine that the project – whatever you're aiming to change in the long term – fails. Work backwards from this eventuality and ask yourself what combination of circumstances led to the failure. This enables you to anticipate challenges ahead and ensure that you have willpower on tap when you need it most.

Know that old habits die hard

Imagine that you press the call button on the lift and the lift fails to arrive. You take the stairs instead and carry on with your day. At least you boost your willpower by getting some exercise! You forget about it, and the next day the lift arrives when summoned. The day after that, however, the lift once again fails to arrive. This erratic pattern continues: lift some days; stairs, of necessity, on other days.

How long do you persevere with pressing the call button, bearing in mind that a no-show by the lift means wasting time waiting when you could be using the stairs? My guess is that within days you simply use the stairs. You quickly learn that the effort of pressing the button and the cost of waiting isn't rewarded by the arrival of the lift. In effect, the behaviour's no longer associated with any value and fades away. You require little if any willpower to resist the urge to press that button.

Motivated habits – behaviours that are driven by strong appetites, say for food, sex or drugs – cast a longer shadow, however, and are not easily forgotten.

Beware of old appetites

Imagine that you quit smoking, cut your losses and quit gambling, or decide to forego your favourite sugar-laced dessert. You're doing well. Your health and bank balance improve accordingly. The years pass and everything's fine until one day you're caught off-guard and find yourself about to light up, place a bet or scoff a pudding. Like an old flame, the desire endures. This is despite successfully resisting the trigger for years.

Appetitive or pleasure-related cues hold their value, unlike more mundane triggers. This may be because, in the natural world, which shaped human development through evolution, survival often depended on having a long memory for cues that predicted rewards associated with food or sex. Both of these were available in an unpredictable way, so a long memory was advantageous. The person who hesitated or forgot missed out and joined the list of hungry or the dead, because rewards exist to promote survival.

Triggers like these can grab your attention automatically, so may play havoc with your willpower.

Don't let losses lead you

When you devote time or energy towards overcoming an unwanted habit or striving for a valued goal, you're an investor. Similar to investing in stocks or shares, you want a return on your outlay of effort. Economists call this phenomenon *sunk costs*.

A simple example in everyday life is spending ten minutes waiting for a bus. Because you've 'invested' something of value – your time – the decision to turn on your heel and walk home is made difficult. However, the 'cost' represented by the effort of walking – perhaps when you're feeling tired or it's raining and you'll get wet – remains the same. Eventually, if the bus fails to show, you'll be obliged to walk home with your willpower depleted because of the frustration of waiting longer in an effort to justify your initial investment.

People are motivated to avoid and mitigate losses because they are loss averse. This 'loss hurts' principle states that losing £10 causes more irritation than finding £10 leads to satisfaction (unless the £10 you find is the note you lost, which acquires added value when you discover it!). Similarly, after a successful fishing expedition, anglers talk about the 'one that got away'.

In the long term, not wanting to lose can lead to the futile pursuit of a goal that's no longer attainable. This can drain your willpower. Sometimes, the goalposts move and you're better off accepting that.

Don't be complacent!

You have a long memory for what was once a source of pleasure and reward. This means that you can never allow yourself to become complacent in the months or even years following a decision to quit smoking or change your diet. Clearly, the longer you sustain change, the more likely you are to continue doing so: success breeds success. But your success is often due to the fact that you get more skilled at making choices and successfully changing your lifestyle and thus avoiding temptation.

Lifestyle change and avoiding temptation are both good ways to support willpower, but the remembrance of rewards past is a potential pitfall. Moreover, this memory is an unconscious memory. Although you may sincerely agree with the statement, 'Cigarettes, I don't even like them, so there's no risk of me lighting up,' an unconscious part of you – your memory for rewards – has a more simple mantra, 'I want a cigarette, and I want it now.' This is reminiscent of what was reputedly said of the Bourbon rulers when they were reinstated and almost provoked a second French revolution: 'They have learned nothing and they have forgotten nothing.' In order to sustain change over time, you could do well to remember those words or the even simpler message, 'Old habits die hard.'

Chapter 6

Know Your Triggers! Forewarned is Forearmed

*I*n this chapter, I emphasise the importance of recognising the triggers that drive your habits and thus challenge your willpower. An unidentified trigger can sabotage your willpower, but recognising triggers helps put you back in the driving seat. This enables you to say no when offered a cigarette or yes when a friend suggests you join her fitness class. Your willpower is vulnerable to challenges, so anticipation and preparation are essential if you are to maintain your goals.

Habits, whether carrying on doing something you want to stop, or repeatedly avoiding something you really need to finish, are hard to break. But their greatest strength is also their greatest weakness. Habits are predictable. This predictability gives you a crucial advantage: it enables you to plan and rehearse ways to maintain change.

Identifying Your Triggers

Some years ago one of my clients, I'll call her Susan, quit drinking alcohol because she knew it was having a negative effect on her health and well-being. She did really well to begin with, until, that is, she went to visit her in-laws with her husband. They had tactfully placed any alcohol out of sight. In the spare room, however, in the cupboard, Susan discovered a bottle of vodka she'd hidden some months earlier. She immediately opened it and started to gulp down the contents. This example is what I mean by a willpower ambush. Susan hadn't anticipated finding the vodka, and thus had no chance to plan a coping strategy.

Similarly, you need to anticipate the triggers that might ambush your willpower. These can be triggers for alcohol, food, sex or tobacco, or just an urge to do nothing when you really need to make an effort. Triggers often appear to come out of the blue, but that's because you didn't identify them as triggers ahead of time.

Recognising your internal and external triggers

Triggers come in all shapes and sizes but can be divided into two categories:

- ✔ **External:** People, places and things
- ✔ **Internal:** Moods, thoughts and cravings

Triggers of either type can challenge your willpower. The good news is that you have a powerful weapon to disarm these triggers: identifying them in advance and rehearsing how to deal with them.

Coping with internal triggers

An *internal trigger* can be a thought, a feeling or a physical sensation. Almost always, it's a combination of these. For example, you may feel hungry, recall that there's a chocolate bar in the drawer, and reach out for it.

On its own, the trigger is just a signal; it takes motivation to act on it. That gives you vital seconds to recruit your willpower. Recognising the link between the trigger and the action of eating a sugary snack – which may not be what you *really* want – enables you to use your willpower to good effect by getting it to do what it's good at: planning.

So, if you recognise that hunger pangs are a trigger and you often feel hungry mid-morning, you can plan a coping strategy such as to eat a proper breakfast, sip water when you feel hungry, or simply not store bars of chocolate in your desk! You can also challenge the thought, 'I need food.' You may well be hungry, or just craving something sweet, but healthy adults can and do survive without food for lengthy periods, certainly more than the hour or so until lunch in this scenario!

These strategies are not, of course, guaranteed to work. You're much more likely to cope with the trigger by knowing in advance that you're going to encounter it, however. Forward planning is one of the best ways to get the most from your willpower. Your willpower doesn't cope well with surprises.

Adjusting to external triggers

External triggers are the things, places or people that can activate and guide your behaviour. These can be very helpful, even essential – for example, a green light signalling you to put your foot on the accelerator, and a red light telling you to stop. Experienced drivers respond to traffic signals without thinking. This response is good for driving, but not always so good when triggers linked to food, sex or drug taking grab your attention and you find yourself acting on impulse. Because triggers act fast, they can outsmart your willpower.

The vanishing heroin addicts

In the dark days of the Vietnam War, heroin was widely used and abused by US soldiers. The Veterans Administration anticipated an influx of heroin addicts as the troops were repatriated, but the detoxification and rehabilitation centres experienced a mere trickle of admissions rather than the anticipated flood.

Doctors came to understand that the addiction was fuelled by the sights and sounds of war in the jungles of Southeast Asia and quickly faded when solders went home to a completely different environment. This shows that addiction, the most potent challenge to willpower, is strongly influenced by environmental or situational triggers.

Recognising the triggers that activate your own habits and impulses is essential for you to use your willpower to override them. This allows you to plan a coping strategy in advance, or simply to decide to avoid the trigger if you think it will be too much of a challenge for your willpower.

For example, say your intention is to stop drinking alcohol. You walk past an off licence on your way home from work. One day, you see your favourite wine on sale. If you don't have a plan in place, you may succumb to temptation, go into the shop, buy a couple of bottles, and end up drinking one that night. However, if you recognise that the advert in the shop window is a trigger, you can use different route to walk home from work, make other plans for the evening, or focus on trying out a new recipe at home.

Being prepared

Before any aircraft takes off, passengers always get a safety briefing from the cabin staff or on the aircraft's video system. Emergency exits are pointed out, passengers are reminded to comply with the seatbelt directions, and evacuation procedures are described 'in the unlikely event of an emergency landing'. This is because if an emergency happens, it's too late to practise!

Your willpower is a powerful ally, but it doesn't respond immediately when confronted with sudden or unexpected challenges. If you prepare and rehearse a plan in advance, your willpower has vital seconds in which to come to your aid. Thus prepared, it can mobilise effective coping strategies, particularly in the face of strong impulses, urges or cravings.

Recognising your triggers early buys you valuable time to select and use coping skills. Habits have long memories that are easily triggered. Because the triggers can be subtle, you can easily miss them and sleep-walk back into old habits.

You may think that foregoing the diet, cancelling the trip to the gym, or picking up a cigarette after weeks of abstaining is just down to bad luck or chance. It isn't! Your brain is incapable of random thought, and you're incapable of random actions. Try listing random numbers from, say, 0 to 50. Most people start with low numbers, but random numbers can be 32, 2, 20, 10, 14, 18, 24. You can't be random, even if you have limitless willpower. You can, of course, act irrationally and impulsively, contrary to your willpower goal. The best way to counteract this is to anticipate the triggers and be prepared to deal with them.

The first step is to recognise your triggers. First ask yourself, 'When did I last eat too much, drink too much, delay finishing a piece of work for no real reason, have sex when it was better not to?' (Feel free to come up with other examples!) Next, take Table 6-1 and identify your triggers: where were you, what caught your attention, who were you with? This is not about guilt, regret or remorse; it's about recognising *appetitive triggers* – those that give you a green light to indulge – so that you can choose differently next time you encounter them, as you inevitably will.

To get you started, I've provided an example in the first row. Your task is to recall times when you've acted on impulse by choosing an immediate smaller reward rather than holding out for a delayed but larger reward. (You discover more about how to use rewards to boost your willpower in Chapter 8, but here it's important to recognise how the lure of instant rewards can derail your willpower.) Identifying your tempting triggers in advance is the single most important thing you can do to cope with them. This primes your willpower to kick into action when the chips are down.

I suggest that you identify just three tempting triggers because I don't want you to overload your working memory or your willpower. If you're trying to anticipate too many temptations, you risk overwhelming your willpower. Consider prioritising your goals, and anticipate your temptations accordingly. Remember that triggers can be internal states such as hunger, sexual desire or tiredness, or external cues such as signs saying 'happy hour' or 'buy one drink, get one free' in a pub.

Triggers are often situational or contextual – in effect a combination of internal and external, for example feeling tired or stressed and seeing the inviting sign in the pub. As you rush by the pub in the morning, you're less likely to notice or respond to the sign, but if you've had a stressful day at work, the trigger can be more noticeable and compelling.

Table 6-1	Three Tempting Triggers		
Trigger	*Time and Place*	*Rating 0–10*	*Outcome*
Example: My new tablet with *Clash of Clans* installed	11 p.m. in bed	8	Spend two hours playing online, spend £12, and oversleep the next day. Feel tired the next day, too, and am not very productive at work.
Trigger 1:			
Trigger 2:			
Trigger 3:			

 Impulsive actions aren't random actions! The impulses that are the greatest challenge to your willpower don't usually come out of the blue. They can be sudden, undoubtedly, but if you look for triggers you can usually find them. This means that your willpower is less likely to be caught off guard.

Planning to Cope

Remembering to do something in the future is called *prospective memory*. It's what the cabin crew are trying to tap into when they do the airplane safety drill yet again. Prospective memory is quite different from recalling what you had for breakfast, which was in the past and is *retrospective memory*. Prospective memory in the context of your breakfast is, 'I must remember to have two eggs tomorrow, because I'll be having a late lunch.' In common with the two strategies I describe in the following sections – 'if, then' and 'now, later' – here you're making a future investment in your willpower. By anticipating challenges to your willpower and linking an action to a trigger, you can reduce the chance of being taken by surprise (willpower doesn't like surprises!) and increase the likelihood of coping effectively. It also makes more efficient use of your willpower. You make a small effort by planning in advance, so that fewer demands are made on your willpower in the heat of the moment.

More mundane examples include telling yourself, 'The next time I'm in supermarket, I must remember to buy some light bulbs.' This is a form of event-based prospective memory, because it links an event (shopping) with a planned or intended action (buying light bulbs). The other type of prospective memory is time based, for example remembering to water a houseplant once a week. I tended to forget this task until I created a prospective memory which went something like, 'Every Sunday, I must remember to water my houseplant.' As I write this chapter on Saturday, it seems much more likely that I'll remember to water my low-maintenance kentia palm tomorrow. By the way, I also need light bulbs! These two scenarios illustrate how associating a planned or necessary action with an event or a time can help ensure that things get done.

Remembering to buy light bulbs and to water plants doesn't require much willpower, but when the temptation to revert to old habits occurs, those urges can often overwhelm your willpower, making your mind go blank. Remembering the future is a vital willpower tool when encountering these challenges to your resolve or your goals. It's like putting some willpower in the bank to be withdrawn when needed.

The old saying that 'the road to hell is paved with good intentions' means that your well-intentioned efforts often fail due to lack of willpower. For every hundred smokers who initially quit, only five go on to remain smoke-free five years later.

An intention is necessary but not sufficient to carry out and sustain a planned behaviour. To succeed, you need a plan or *implementation strategy* for the intention. This provides an opportunity to rephrase the old adage to, 'The road to health is paved with good rehearsals'! With regard to quitting smoking, rehearsing your plan can be as simple as telling yourself, 'If I'm offered a cigarette, I'll say, "No thanks, I've quit."'

Rehearsing your response in the face of a trigger, which I talk about earlier in this chapter, reduces the mental effort you need to resist temptation, and thus preserves your supply of willpower needed to control the impulse in the moment.

Bearing in mind that a newly abstaining smoker might be offered cigarettes several times in the course of a social gathering, a coping strategy that promotes economical use of willpower comes highly recommended! Your willpower is a limited resource.

You don't need to use your willpower all the time; this would be wasteful, like keeping your motor running when your car is parked in the driveway. The secret to maximising your willpower is to make sure it's available when and where you need it most.

Whether you're harnessing willpower to pursue a long-term goal or to suppress a long-standing habit, you'll encounter situations in which you need to draw on your willpower. This book aims to show you how to build reserves of accessible willpower.

Putting the 'if, then' strategy to use

When you use your willpower to change your behaviour, tension arises between the old behaviour and the new. This reaches a peak when you encounter a trigger associated with the old pattern. It's like bumping into an old flame – despite the time elapsed, the longing endures. The new behaviour can be undermined by the old impulse.

The trigger can be fast tracked by your impulsive brain, and you can find yourself picking up that cigarette, opting for the cheesecake rather than the fruit salad, or exchanging phone numbers with the old flame! Formulating a simple plan in advance greatly improves your chance of achieving your long-term goal. If you have to think of a plan in the heat of the moment, you use more willpower than you really need to, or simply fall victim to the IGNWL (I've got no willpower left) syndrome. The simple 'if, then' approach is a game plan that buys you valuable time when your willpower encounters 'I want it now' moments.

Formulating an 'if, then' strategy builds on the exercise in Table 6-1. Identifying the triggers for your impulsive moments is part of the solution, providing you with more awareness. Recognising triggers is necessary, but not sufficient, to overcome impulses: you also need tactics, which is what the 'if, then' approach is all about. Being forewarned is much more useful if you're forearmed as well.

Table 6-2 shows examples of the 'if, then' strategy in use.

Table 6-2	Example 'If, Then' Strategies
Goal	*'If, Then' Plan*
Drink less	If I'm offered a large glass of wine, **then** I'll say, 'I'd love a small glass of wine and a glass of water as well.'
Exercise more	If I see a Zumba class advertised, **then** I'll book a place.
Quit smoking	If I'm offered a cigarette, **then** I'll say, 'No thanks, I've quit.'

Acting on the 'now versus later' strategy

Another effective coping strategy is to compare the immediate consequences of acting impulsively with the delayed consequences – using the 'now versus later' strategy. This helps overcome the 'smaller sooner' versus 'larger later' dilemma that everyone encounters from time to time.

Think about it. You need willpower to keep focused on the longer term. Save some money this month, and you can have a better holiday in six months, for example. Focusing on the longer term is easier said than done, though – this book doesn't need a section about overcoming impulses to rush to the bank and deposit the money that you could have spent on a fun night out! You need willpower more to focus on the greater benefits that come over time (the larger, later reward of the holiday or weight loss, for example) rather than the smaller, sooner rewards of clubbing or an indulgent meal that are tantalisingly within reach.

The 'now versus later' strategy helps you focus directly on the costs and benefits of immediate gratification versus pleasure postponed. This strategy isn't intended to steer you to a bread and water diet, or indeed towards a lifestyle of perpetual indulgence! That said, the example of smoking or not smoking, below, should be a no-brainer. Overall, the 'now versus later' technique can help you use your willpower to make informed choices and achieve the right balance between immediate gratification and delayed reward.

This strategy works in two ways:

✔ **It enables you to re-evaluate the pros and cons of the decision at hand.** Staying in bed for another 15 minutes may feel good at the moment, but it may mean you miss out on a seat on the train and arrive at work feeling tired (and perhaps looking sheepish because you're late!).

✔ **It disengages your impulsive brain system.** Your impulsive brain is the part that says, 'I want it now.' If you pause to consider your action, you activate a more reflective brain system that can look further ahead – the 'it would be nice to stay in bed now, but my aim is to get to work early' bit.

Of course, your willpower is based in the more contemplative part of your brain, so this strategy summons this great resource.

Table 6-3 shows examples of 'now versus later' strategy in action.

Table 6-3	The 'Now Versus Later' Strategy and Quitting Smoking	
	Immediate Consequences: Now	*Long-term Consequences: Later*
Positive Expectations	I'll feel included, part of the crowd; sheer pleasure; less boredom.	None! That's why I decided to quit!
Negative Expectations	I'll feel disappointed with myself; my breath will smell when I get home.	I may get cancer or some other illness and die! I'll have wasted my money.

Forming and Changing Habits

Doing anything for the first time – whether it's smoking a cigarette, sampling alcohol or another drug, or deciding to sit down and watch a television show – usually reflects a conscious choice. With repetition, the element of choice reduces, the behaviour becomes automatic, and a habit is born.

_____ **Chapter 6: Know Your Triggers! Forewarned is Forearmed** *89*

Promptings for new habits – and old ones

I changed jobs a few years ago. This meant relocating from suburban west London to Covent Garden, in central London. Soon, friends and colleagues began to comment on my new trendy image: the smart shoes, the sharp suits and the trendy shirts. In west London, I worked near my health club, and two or three times a week I headed straight there after work. In Covent Garden, in contrast, my journey home involved walking past some of the coolest shops in London. My acquisition of more shoes and more shirts than I really needed wasn't evidence of a midlife crisis (I bought the sports car five years earlier!), but simply a response to a different environment containing different triggers.

A few months after I moved jobs, I was absentmindedly browsing in yet another shoe shop when I realised that I hadn't been jogging for nearly a week. To my surprise, I experienced an urge to head for home in order to go for a run. I then realised that I was standing next to a display of trainers. Finally, it seemed that a shopping trigger had propelled me out of the store, and without my credit card seeing the light of day. While triggers can often challenge your resolve and undermine your willpower, they sometimes provide a nudge in the right direction.

Forming habits can be very helpful: it frees up thinking space. Recall your first driving lesson, for example. You carried out the complex list of procedures involved in operating the vehicle and proceeding safely, such as 'mirror, signal, manoeuver', slowly and deliberately. After a few weeks or months of practice, however, your driving became much more fluent and automatic.

Habits require little if any willpower to carry on, but a large amount of willpower to stop.

Habits become increasingly automatic or instinctive over time. They can be triggered by cues or signals literally before you know what you're doing. Smokers and heavy drinkers, for example, become focused on these triggers in fractions of seconds (about three-hundredths of a second, to be precise!). This triggers impulsive behaviour such as reaching for a cigarette or a drink unconsciously. This unconscious aspect of habits is why overcoming them is challenging to willpower: your willpower is useless until you're consciously aware of what you're doing.

Retraining habits: A case study

Louisa was a successful management consultant who came to see me because she was drinking a bottle of wine a day during the week and two bottles of wine a day at the weekend.

The first step was to clarify her goal and motives. Her aim was to reduce her drinking to sensible levels, perhaps two to three small glasses of wine three or four times a week. Her interim goal was to have two alcohol-free days in the next week. Her motives were to:

✔ Be viewed as a sober and competent professional

✔ Reduce the health risks associated with excessive drinking

✔ Become more clearheaded and focused in order to develop professional work and provide for the future

Establishing goals and motives are necessary but not sufficient in order to overcome habits. Louisa and I agreed that reducing her drinking would take some time, and first she needed to learn the basics of overcoming the habitual aspects of her drinking, a pattern that she'd maintained for 26 years or so.

Louisa agreed to keep a record of her drinking on a daily basis. This revealed that on a Saturday she would sometimes have her first glass of wine shortly after breakfast, as early as 11 a.m. The preceding thought was, 'I have nothing to do and I've nothing arranged, I may as well have a drink.'

We agreed an alternative plan, formulated as an implementation strategy: 'When I wake up next Saturday, I'll have a light breakfast and then I'll go for a swim.' The next Saturday, Louisa didn't have her first glass of wine until 5.30 p.m.

The other trigger that emerged from the diary was excessive drinking in social situations. The strategy devised to tackle this was for Louisa to pick up and drink from her wine glass with her non-dominant (left) hand, while using the dominant (right) hand to sip water.

To be fair to yourself, you can't really shoulder the blame for something you do unconsciously, but you do need to make a careful note of the trigger in order to reduce the chances of it happening again. Sometimes, you can only be wise after the event.

The good news is that if you develop positive habits, say routinely exercising or automatically choosing healthy foods, the same rule applies: you require little willpower to maintain these good habits, but have to make an effort to reverse them. Developing good habits frees up willpower for other uses as well as making it much easier for you to maintain the changes in behaviour and lifestyle that the good habits represent.

Achieving your willpower goals through developing new habits is the key to long-term success. This also frees up willpower for other purposes and new challenges.

To establish a new habit, use these tips:

- ✔ **Develop a routine.** Exercise at the same time on the same days every week; assign particular timeslots to work or study on particular projects.

- ✔ **Reward yourself.** Identify a reward or treat to enjoy after you've completed the behaviour you want to make habitual.

- ✔ **Keep a record of the behaviour.** For example, keep a journal of the distance you run each day, the time you spend exercising, or the number of words you write for your school or work project. (Make this easy for yourself by using a smartphone app for logging exercise or recording calories, or monitoring the word count on your word-processing software.)

Chapter 7

Be Kind to Yourself When You Fail

▶ Accepting responsibility without blaming yourself

▶ Using setbacks to refocus on your goal

---

*Y*our goals are important and give meaning to your life. That's why you chose to invest willpower in pursuing them. This chapter imparts the key message that how you respond to the inevitable setbacks determines whether you succeed or fail in the long term. As Oscar Wilde said so succinctly, 'Experience is the name we give to our mistakes.'

When you stumble while trying to achieve your goals, you often trigger self-criticism and self-blame. In this chapter, I show you how to recognise and avoid the blaming trap and the negative feelings that follow. Negative feelings can further sap your willpower and reduce your motivation to learn from the experience of the setback and to reset your goals.

Taking Responsibility While Avoiding Self-blame

Engaging willpower to pursue important and valued goals always involves trial and error. Blaming yourself for inevitable failures can trigger negative emotions and further deplete your willpower and motivation. The aim is to avoid the blame game and instead learn from the experience while accepting that things didn't go according to plan. This is the best way to reboot your willpower!

After a setback, in order to preserve your willpower and sustain your motivation, you need to focus on learning lessons, managing your negative emotions and identifying new ways of coping.

When you choose an ambitious path or goal, the risk of failure increases. After all, using willpower to pursue goals that *aren't* meaningful or to follow plans that *lack* value and ambition is a waste of a precious resource.

Accepting the responsibility to do better

Accepting responsibility enables you to accept credit when it's due, and gives you an opportunity to learn from your mistakes. This accountability is crucial for building the strength of your willpower and compensating for areas of weakness. However, you need to be on your guard against two common thinking traps:

- ✔ Discounting or explaining away your own shortcomings.

  For example, you arrive late for a meeting and mumble, 'Sorry, I got stuck in traffic.' Or consider the situation when you drink more than you intended to and, on arriving home, tell your partner this was because there was a happy hour in the pub, with an apparently irresistible 'buy one, get one free' deal. In both scenarios, responsibility is neatly sidestepped, thus reducing any opportunity to learn lessons such as anticipating the morning rush-hour or skipping the happy hour.

- ✔ Downplaying personal responsibility for your achievements. One of the key themes of this book is that you should reward yourself for effort and achievement. Doing so is vital for reinforcing your willpower. Sometimes, though, people display a reluctance to accept credit or praise for their achievements.

  For example, if you obtain excellent GCSE grades, the result of years of willpower-driven effort, you might account for it by saying that you had excellent teachers or went to a very good school. True, these are key ingredients in your success, but discounting your own considerable contribution risks limiting your expression of willpower in the future, because you've not fully valued it in the present.

If you find that these thinking patterns apply to you, check out Chapter 10 and discover more about the power of accepting personal responsibility.

Seeing failure as an opportunity for change

If you're aiming to achieve long-term change using willpower, you inevitably encounter occasional setbacks. If these setbacks leave you feeling bereft and demoralised, you risk squandering the precious willpower you've already invested.

Discovering ways to deal positively with failure and setbacks is vital, which makes this one of the most important chapters in the book. Although sometimes failure seems inevitable, you can find different ways to respond to it. In particular, that you emerge from a setback with your willpower intact, or at least ready to be recharged, is vital!

If you get things right every time, you never learn anything new. You simply carry on doing the same thing the same way. How dull is that? As the saying goes, never waste a good crisis. Seriously, tripping up or failing is a great opportunity for learning.

Benefiting from your mistakes may entail facing up to some home truths, but ultimately is about taking responsibility and learning lessons rather than blaming yourself or putting yourself down. The message: reward yourself for your effort and learn from your mistakes.

Forgoing self-blame

Typically, when things go wrong – whether it's a traffic accident, a large corporation going bankrupt or a government losing an election – the first question asked is, 'Who's to blame?' Assigning blame or causality can be a complex process, with blame being shared generously!

If you're harnessing willpower to achieve your goal, it's a bit more personal – and it's all too easy to point the accusatory finger at yourself! After all, you're the one who gave in to temptation or couldn't summon up the motivation to go to the gym for the last three weeks.

Any endeavour that requires willpower – whether quitting smoking, sticking to that diet or following the latest exercise regime – is prone to setbacks. When you face a setback, you can sometimes be your own worst enemy. If you can learn lessons that may prevent a recurrence of the unwanted event, all well and good. Benefiting from your mistakes is an important component of using willpower to achieve your goals.

The problem with blaming is that pointing the finger, in this case at yourself, isn't usually very enlightening! Thoughts such as 'I'm useless' or 'I failed again,' or simply 'It's all my fault,' don't give you the chance to learn from the setback. On the contrary, by triggering feelings of guilt or shame, this self-critical, accusatory style of thinking can drain your motivation and deplete your willpower. This is your hot, emotional brain in the driving seat.

In order to benefit from setbacks and mistakes, you need to get your hot, emotional brain out of the driving seat and engage your cool, reflective brain instead. This can enable you to plan ahead and reduce the risk of repeating the same mistakes.

Losing hurts

You've probably mislaid a small amount of money, say £20, at some stage. You may also have found £20 (perhaps the same banknote!) in an old pair of jeans. My guess is that the negative feelings following the realisation of the loss were more pronounced than the positive feelings you experienced at the discovery of the freshly laundered banknote. Research backs me up on this, showing that people are, in fact, more sensitive to losses than to gains. A typical study shows that participants in an experiment invest more effort to prevent losses than to secure equivalent gains.

When you decide to channel your willpower in pursuit of a given goal, you invest value in the goal. When you lose something of value, it hurts! Psychologists call this the *goal violation effect* or the *rule violation effect*. You experience this effect as regret or remorse and self-blame when your willpower proves insufficient and you succumb to temptation. The trademark thoughts are, 'I'm weak, I'll probably stay that way, and this will affect me in many ways.' This makes it more likely that a lapse – for example, smoking one cigarette after two weeks or abandoning your keep-fit programme for a day or two – will become a full-blown relapse: you quit quitting or you quit trying.

Mirror neurons

When you simply *observe* somebody doing something such as running or smiling, specialist brain cells become active, as if you were carrying out the action yourself. This is due to brain cells known as *mirror neurons*. These remarkable cells seem to adopt the other person's point of view; if I watch somebody reach out and grab an apple, for example, the mirror neurons will activate as if I'm grabbing the fruit!

Another type of mirror neuron is exquisitely sensitive to touch. This is why watching a movie can be so involving – your mirror neurons light up when the actors touch lovingly, and you flinch when your hero gets clobbered. This capacity is innate – even newly born infants are good mimics.

Activating mirror neurons requires little if any willpower – it is automatic. Brain scientists believe that these cells enable people to learn, communicate and empathise more effectively. (Children diagnosed with autism – key features of which are difficulties in empathising and communicating – appear to have deficient mirror neurons.) Normally, however, it appears that when you're kind and considerate to other people, your mirror neurons are activated, so you feel the love!

The best way to overcome the guilt that comes with breaking your own rules is to change your thinking. Try, for example, thinking, 'I had a moment of weakness, I'll probably have more, but one swallow doesn't make a summer.'

If you slip up when pursuing a long-term goal, be that when quitting smoking or trying to stick to your diet or exercise regime, recognise it as a lapse rather than a complete failure.

Negative emotions can further deplete your willpower. (I explain this more fully in Chapter 2.) This can make a drama out of a crisis. For example, if your goal is to cut down or quit using alcohol, breaking this rule can be associated with negative emotions such as guilt or shame. These unpleasant feelings can trigger further heavy drinking.

If you gamble, you inevitably have losses as well as wins. The negative feelings you experience after losing can trigger more gambling in an effort to regain the money you lost. This can set up a vicious circle of further losses and further futile gambling. *Chasing losses,* as this pattern is called, is a clear warning that you may be at risk of becoming a problem gambler. If you gamble, set a limit on how much you can afford to lose. When you reach that amount, stop gambling. The negative feelings will pass!

Recovering from a Setback

Any endeavour that requires willpower – whether quitting smoking, sticking to that diet or following the latest exercise regime – is prone to setbacks.

When you face a setback, as you almost certainly will, you need to look for lessons that can help prevent a recurrence of the unwanted event. Benefiting from your mistakes is an important component of using willpower to achieve your goals. Nobody invites setbacks or likes a plan to fail. However, you can respond to failure in different ways. Being kind to yourself and avoiding self-blame is the best way to foster the resilience you need to move on from the setback.

 Positive emotions create a mindset within which willpower will flourish, while negative feelings compete for your limited supply of willpower. Carrying out an act of kindness to an individual less fortunate than you can make you feel good, too! Expressing empathy and compassion for others can make you more self-aware and activate loving kindness towards yourself (see the 'Mirror neurons' sidebar).

Switching your perspective

Blame, like beauty, is in the eye of the beholder. It is subjective – an interpretation of events. You can always find an alternative interpretation that emphasises the lessons learned rather than the blame attributed.

A narrow, self-blaming response can deplete your willpower and jeopardise reaching your goal. Alternatively, you can come up with a more constructive appraisal that emphasises learning from your mistakes and planning strategies to triumph the next time you find yourself in a similar situation. This more nuanced response increases the likelihood of persistent effort. Another word for persistent effort is – you guessed it! – willpower.

Joanna's smoking hot night out

Joanna had stuck diligently to her New Year's resolution to quit smoking – until 25 January, that is. That fateful Friday night, she went out after work with some friends who were smokers.

After Joanna had drunk two glasses of wine, the friends announced they were going outside to smoke and invited Joanna to join them. Joanna smoked three cigarettes with them that evening and purchased a pack on the way home. When she got home, she smoked two more.

The following list outlines how Joanna can blame herself and deplete her willpower, or she can come up with a more constructive appraisal and plan her next steps and responses. The two contrasting responses are:

✔ **Willpower-sapping, blaming response:** Typical! I'm so weak! I have no willpower.

Consequence: I feel bad about myself. I feel like having another cigarette! There's no point trying to quit, I'll just buy a pack of cigarettes.

✔ **Willpower-maintaining, adaptive response:** Quitting is proving harder than I thought. I took my eye off the ball. My willpower kept me going for over three weeks.

Consequence: I need to be on my guard when I go out with the sales team. After a stressful week at work, my supply of willpower had dwindled. The wine didn't help!

Managing negative thoughts

When Homer Simpson screws things up, he utters his catchphrase 'd'oh' before cheerfully moving on to cause more problems for himself and the long-suffering Simpson family. When things go wrong in real life, however, you can end up feeling bad about yourself.

Because your memories are stored in your neural networks, the experience of failure brings to mind other occasions when things didn't work out. You can deal with these memories in two ways:

✔ Challenge or re-evaluate your thoughts and memories of past failures.

✔ Accept the thoughts simply as thoughts that have no power or relevance here and now.

The next sections explain both options and point out the strengths of each.

Challenging your thoughts

Before the mid-16th century, it seemed obvious that the Sun revolved around the Earth. Of course, the astronomer Copernicus proved this belief to be wrong and illusory. It *felt* true, however. This emotional flavour invests thoughts with a false sense of credibility. Thoughts such as 'I'm a failure,' 'I can't do anything right' or 'I have no willpower' may appear plausible in the moment, but are neither true nor helpful.

The key question is, 'Where's the evidence?' The quest for evidence, after all, prompted Copernicus to point his telescope at the sky.

To challenge the belief 'I can't do anything right,' all you need to do is think of one example of when you did do something right and achieved your purpose.

Table 7-1 shows examples of how to find evidence to balance your thoughts about your abilities.

Table 7-1	Going with the Evidence	
Evidence to Support the Thought, 'I Can't Do Anything Right'	**Evidence that Contradicts the Thought, 'I Can't Do Anything Right'**	**Conclusion**
I didn't deliver the project on time.	I completed two projects on time last year.	I don't always get things right, but I seem to have found the right level of challenge in the projects I undertake. That said, I think I could manage my time and priorities a bit better.
This isn't the first time I've missed a deadline.	I identified a flaw in the project plan that necessitated a delay. It wasn't my fault!	
I had to repeat my final year at university.	I was ill for three months of my final year.	

Dismissing a thought as just a thought

Another way of dealing with negative thoughts is to accept them simply as thoughts. At face value, this seems at odds with advice in the preceding section to challenge and dispute them. However, accepting your thoughts is another means of defusing or disempowering them. By accepting that a thought is just a thought, you gain some distance from thoughts that may be fuelling negative emotions which can further deplete your willpower.

Imagery techniques are useful in defusing or distancing negative thoughts. A couple of techniques that are particularly useful in defusing negative thoughts are:

✔ **Poisonous parrot:** For this exercise, you need to visualise a parrot perched on your shoulder (where else?). This angry and spiteful bird has a bad attitude and only ever says negative, nasty things about you, such as, 'You're useless,' 'You're a failure' and 'There you go again!' – no doubt, in between the characteristic squawks! But the parrot is not you, it's only sitting on you. You can therefore create some distance between yourself and the parrot's negative narrative. It's just a parrot after all, and you can put it back in a cage and either cover the cage or leave the room.

✔ **Flowing river:** In this visual technique, you imagine yourself sitting on the bank of a river. You cast your negative thoughts onto the water and visualise them floating downstream, away from you.

Both these imagery techniques enable you to disengage from unhelpful thoughts and curtail any negative emotions associated with them. By regulating your emotions, you preserve your supply of willpower.

Choosing to challenge or accept

Whether it's best to challenge or accept a thought depends on the thought. Some negative thoughts lend themselves to challenge.

When you take time to reflect about a specific incident – after your brain circuits have cooled down – you can usually easily recall an episode of success or achievement and thereby discount the self-directed accusations of failure or ineptitude.

More general and vague negative thoughts such as, 'What's the point?', 'Why bother?' and 'This is useless' are harder to challenge. This type of general negativity can really puncture your willpower balloon! If pursuing a goal is pointless, willpower becomes redundant. Moreover, challenging these thoughts can sometimes lead to hollow philosophical debate, such as questioning the meaning of life. Accordingly, recognising that 'This is pointless' is just a thought and nothing more enables you to dispatch it downstream.

An important consideration is that acceptance and emotional defusing techniques generally require less willpower than systematically weighing up the evidence that supports or discounts the particular thought. If you experience a setback due to lack of willpower, you need to restore your vital reserves as quickly as possible. Acceptance rather than challenge may well be a more economical way – by which I mean that you spend less willpower – of dealing with negative thoughts and the negative emotions that they trigger. This conserves your limited supply of willpower.

Some thoughts and beliefs about aspects of yourself – for example, that you're unattractive or unlovable, or in some way unworthy or incompetent – can prove more difficult to discount, as well as being quite distressing. These self-evaluations can become more prominent in the face of setbacks or failure. If you find you can't get rid of these beliefs and your mood remains low day after day, consult your doctor or a psychotherapist.

Restoring your confidence

If you experience a setback because you're unable to summon up sufficient willpower, your self-confidence may dip. Your memory stores examples of failure in connected networks: experience one failure, and other failures are likely to come to mind.

When such setbacks happen, try reminding yourself of a satisfying achievement in your life or a valued role you played. This may require some effort – and thus willpower – but recalling past success is a good use of your scarce willpower resource. Reflecting on earlier achievements can reset your self-confidence to its rightful level! And self-confidence is vital in order to refocus on your goal.

Developing an internal critic – Susan's story

The tendency to respond to setbacks by being excessively self-critical is likely to stem from a combination of personality characteristics such as conscientiousness (one of the Big Five described in Chapter 2) and the nature of early relationships with parents, teachers, siblings and peers.

Parents who are overcritical and perhaps set relentlessly high standards can trigger comparable perfectionist traits in their children. For example, a client, I'll call her Susan, told me that when she was a child, even if she did really well at school,

coming second or third in the class, her mother would ask, 'Why not first?' As a result, Susan never felt truly valued unless she excelled.

When Susan started working, this feeling of never being quite good enough unless she was the best performer on her team recurred. This created a vicious circle whereby Susan set unrealistically high goals and exhausted her supply of willpower in striving for them. When she failed to attain the objectives, Susan would blame herself, attributing the setback to internal factors such as her perceived weakness.

Re-evaluating and re-setting your goal

If you encounter a roadblock in the quest for your goal, the problem may not be you: it could be the goal that you chose. Ask yourself whether your goal was realistic and specific. An unhelpful way of formulating a goal is, 'I want to be successful/happier/healthier.' More helpful and measurable approaches are, 'I want to complete my training course and achieve a place in the top ten in the class,' 'I want to lose 5 kilograms in the next two months' or 'I'll exercise for 45 minutes three times a week.'

Check out the SMART approach to setting goals in Chapter 5. Your goal may meet the first two SMART criteria and be specific and measurable – quitting smoking or getting promoted at work, for example. I find that these are the more straightforward parts of the goal-setting process. The other components of the SMART approach to goal setting are often where the obstacles lie. You need to question to what degree the goal was attainable, realistic and timely.

Evaluating your goal

Recall a situation where you set yourself a goal – getting a promotion at work, dating somebody new, losing a kilogram in weight or quitting smoking – and didn't achieve it. For illustrative purposes, I assume the goal was promotion at work. A good place to start is by asking to what extent you were really able to influence, never mind determine, the outcome. Career progression is never entirely (and sometimes just never!) under your control. Sure, you can influence it – a good use of willpower – but you need to factor in the competition, your relationship with your seniors, and broader economic factors (nobody gets promoted; nobody gets a pay rise!). Accordingly, while your goal may be specific and measurable, it may not be attainable, realistic or timely.

Resetting your goal

Pressing the reset button after a setback can lead to a revised, possibly intermediate, goal. For the person wanting a promotion, a new interim goal may be, 'I'll get a place on the next relevant training course to ensure I'm an attractive candidate for promotion when the opportunity arises.'

Re-evaluating your goal provides you with a valuable opportunity to reappraise your role in contributing to the outcome. In the example, this entails taking responsibility for misjudging the timing of the career move, but even the most self-critical hesitate before blaming themselves for a global recession that restricted the company's plans for growth. A balanced appraisal of the factors that contributed to the failure to achieve the goal helps you to avoid self-blame and refocus your willpower towards more realistic and attainable objectives.

No matter how many setbacks you encounter when pursuing your goals, you can always give yourself a pat on the back for using your special power – your willpower.

Chapter 8

Rewarding Yourself along the Way

*I*n your quest for self-improvement or greater well-being, you expend effort from the outset, but the undeniable rewards that follow when you successfully achieve your goal may take months or even years to realise. This time lag creates problems if you're aiming to lose weight, because you need to wait weeks or even months for that admiring glance or comment such as, 'Wow, you look stunning!' But your emotional, impulsive brain isn't capable of long-term planning: a reward deferred is a reward denied. Understanding how important rewards are for mobilising your behaviour is vital for strategic deployment of your willpower. In this chapter, I show you how to be your own willpower coach by rewarding yourself for effort and maintaining your motivation in pursuit of your long-term goal.

The time gap between effort and reward is your willpower's Achilles heel. Distant rewards, such as becoming slim, fit, healthy or better educated, are devalued by your impulsive brain, which responds only to immediate rewards. You need to feed the beast! You need to drip-feed your impulsive brain with rewards as you pursue your goal.

Being Your Own Willpower Coach

A good coach offers encouragement from the first day the novice athlete shows up for training on a cold, dark morning, long before the athlete has any prospect of winning a medal. The coach knows that if athletes don't receive rewards, they'll never have an opportunity to go for gold. The wise coach knows that the best way to achieve distant goals is to focus on measurable short-term objectives. Reaching these milestones reinforces your efforts.

Being your own willpower coach doesn't boost your brain capacity or invest you with any special powers, but it does ensure that you maximise the key ingredient of success: willpower.

Making use of the science of rewards

With the discovery of the brain's pleasure centre (see the nearby sidebar, 'Discovering the brain's reward centre'), came research into the connection between pleasure and motivation. Researchers discovered that the brain learns very quickly the cues and triggers that predict pleasure. These stimuli can grab attention in fractions of a second. And the brain seeks to continue the pleasurable sensation and constantly seeks out enjoyable experiences.

The next time you find yourself looking at something appetising (or someone you find appetising!) be aware that this doesn't happen by chance. Your brain's pleasure centre ensures that your reward radar locks onto the signal.

This relentless scanning for rewards is a major challenge to your willpower, because it can activate urges and craving. When you use your willpower to forego a source of reward such as smoking, drinking alcohol, or eating sugary foods, your brain's reward centre goes into overdrive to redress the balance.

Discovering the brain's reward centre

In the 1950s, two scientists at McGill University in Canada, James Olds and Peter Milner, implanted small electrodes in the brains of laboratory rats. They wanted to study levels of arousal in one part of the brain, but their aim wasn't very precise, and instead the electrodes made contact with the nucleus accumbens. This tiny structure buried deep in the brain is common to all mammals including, of course, humans. Olds and Milner had discovered the brain's pleasure centre – the bit of your brain that lights up when a pleasurable reward is delivered or even promised.

The scientists didn't realise what they'd stumbled on initially, having placed understandable but unwarranted faith in their laboratory skills! They quickly noticed two things that gave them that 'aha!' feeling:

✔ When the electrodes were activated, the rats kept returning to the precise location they were in when the tiny electrical charge stimulated their brains.

✔ When given the chance to press a lever that delivered the small pleasurable jolt, the rats pressed the lever again and again – as many as 2,000 times in an hour. They ignored the opportunity for food, water or sex. Without the intervention of laboratory technicians, the rats would collapse or perish.

When you do something pleasurable, part of your brain is activated and releases a powerful neurochemical called *dopamine*. Along with other neurotransmitters such as naturally occurring opioids and serotonin, dopamine is intimately involved in generating the experience of pleasure and reward.

Dopamine activation is particularly associated with craving or simply wanting something really intensely. It could be called the brain's motivational messenger. Crucially, anything associated with triggering dopamine release – a person, place or object – acquires some of the motivational magic of the reward. This is why the laboratory rats returned to the precise part of the cage where they experienced intense pleasure, even though the features of the cage had nothing whatsoever to do with the reward. Applied to humans, this means that ambient cues – say the voice or face of a person linked to cigarette smoking, or even an ashtray – can trigger dopamine release, craving and possibly relapse.

Unless you find an alternative reward, your willpower will be overwhelmed eventually. Fortunately, a reward doesn't need to be large or even tangible. It can be as simple as the satisfaction of ticking the last item on your to-do list and telling yourself 'well done'. Part of the reward process is simply feedback telling you that, yes, you succeeded! Promptly delivered, this rewarding message can prove to be motivational. As your own willpower coach, you should offer verbal rewards at various points throughout your training programme.

When it comes to rewards, timing is crucial. The reward should follow the target behaviour immediately or as soon as is feasible.

The reason why your willpower seems to evaporate when pursuing long-term aims is that the gains are equally long term. The most effective way to deal with this is to ensure that you're realising a regular source of reinforcement or reward as you strive for your long-term goals. Just saying 'well done' to yourself or identifying a pleasurable activity, an activity you're skilled at, or a treat (you're free to use your imagination!) that doesn't conflict with your long-term goal is the key to rewarding your efforts at each step of the way.

Climbing the goal ladder

The goal ladder is a tool to help you achieve your ambitions. Like a real ladder, the goal ladder enables you to reach a distant goal step by step.

The goal ladder has two major advantages:

✔ You break your goal into logical steps (it is, after all, a step ladder!). Taking things in sequence helps keep your long-term goal in mind. This helps prevent distraction or a lack of focus, the enemies of willpower.

✔ You reward yourself at each step rather than only when you finally realise your goal.

To construct your own goal ladder, follow these steps:

1. **Think of a current concern, a problem or something that you want to change, involving the use of willpower.**

   Formulate your goals in positive terms. Try, 'I want to become more healthy and attractive' rather than 'I need to lose weight because I don't look good.' Your willpower works better when you strive for something positive rather than to escape or avoid something negative or unpleasant.

2. **Identify the steps you need to take to move towards achieving your goal.**

   If, for example, your goal is to become more attractive and healthy, you have many ways to attain this – too many, perhaps! Without the goal ladder, you risk becoming distracted by conflicting goals: do you lose weight, change your hairstyle or dress style, or visit the dental hygienist? Willpower works best when focused on one goal: the goal ladder guides you accordingly.

   For instance, adopting a balanced diet is clearly important in pursuing the overarching goal, and the first step on the goal ladder is to prepare healthy meals. Table 8-1 shows possible steps and rewards towards achieving this goal.

Table 8-1   Goal Ladder for Preparing a Meal

Step	Reward
Step 1: Select a tasty recipe.	Congratulate yourself! Or share it with your friends on Facebook. It might attract a few 'like's.
Step 2: Make a shopping list.	Sit down with a cup of coffee and a favourite magazine for 15 minutes. Engaging in a pleasurable activity is a powerful way to reward yourself (see the later 'Using Rewarding Activities to Boost Willpower' section).
Step 3: Go to shop and buy food.	Smile and chat to the friendly shop assistant. Positive social interactions promote well-being, which boosts willpower.
Step 4: Come back home.	Say 'well done', sit down and have a banana! Or indulge yourself in a guilty pleasure (one that doesn't undo the potential benefits of the step towards your goal, or the goal itself).
Step 5: Check the recipe and begin preparing the meal.	Note that the plan is going very well. Consider inviting a friend to join you.
Step 6: Sit down and enjoy the meal!	Savour the food and congratulate yourself (again!).

3. Identify a way to reward or acknowledge your efforts after each step.

Make a list of pleasurable or rewarding activities or treats. The list should include activities that aren't costly in terms of effort (this would compete for your limited supply of willpower), time or money.

Use the info in the preceding section, 'Making use of the science of rewards', to help devise your rewards. Here are some of mine:

- Grabbing a coffee on the way to work

- Buying my favourite satirical magazine

- Taking the over-ground rather than the underground train (it can take ten minutes longer, but is a more pleasant journey at the end of the day!)

- Downloading an old favourite track to my smart-phone (*L.A. Woman* by The Doors!)

- Telling myself that, while I haven't accomplished everything I wanted to do today, I did enough, and it's okay

- Staying in bed late on a Saturday

Make sure your rewards contribute to your motivational matrix, by reinforcing the successful completion of each step.

4. Compose your goal ladder, including rewards.

Sketch a ladder, use the one in Table 8-2 or draw one on the screen of your electronic device, and record the steps you need to take to move towards achieving your goal.

Table 8-2	My Goal Ladder
Description of the Step	*Reward*
Step 1:	
Step 2:	
Step 3:	
Step 4:	

Reward sensitivity: Willpower weakness can become willpower strength

Some people are more sensitive to rewards than others. This is probably down to a combination of personality, parenting and learning experiences. One way that researchers have investigated this is by enabling people to choose between an immediate reward or a deferred reward. (This is a bit like the famous marshmallow experiments described in Chapter 2, where children could choose one marshmallow immediately or have two if they were prepared to wait 15 or 20 minutes. The more impulsive kids ate one immediately; the less impulsive kids were rewarded with two marshmallows.) Small differences, or gradients, in rewards – the offer of £20 immediately compared with £21 in a week's time – don't discriminate between more or less impulsive people. Most of us choose the immediate reward, calculating that waiting another week isn't worth the hassle.

As the gradient increases, say from £20 now compared with £25, £30 or £35 after a week, those with different levels of impulsivity make distinct choices. The more impulsive you are, the more likely you are to take the money and run! This occurs even if you stand to gain £10 or £15 by waiting a week. This is contrived,

like all experiments, but what it really shows is that some people are more motivated by immediate rewards, whether these are financial, sensory or sexual.

Impulsive people seem to be more susceptible to the lure of short-term rewards and less able to defer gratification. The tendency for people to opt for immediate rewards in experiments is predictive of problems regulating appetitive behaviour with regard to drug use, sex or eating. Impulsive people appear to have less willpower – at least the component of willpower involved in controlling impulses.

Impulsivity, or _reward sensitivity_ to give it its technical name, can be turned around to facilitate willpower, but only if a ready supply of alternative rewards is available. Think of it this way: people with less willpower, or who are less skilled in using willpower, can turn the greatest weakness into their greatest strength! Susceptibility to rewards is a two-way street: it makes you more prone to picking up bad habits, but it should also make it easier to adopt new habits as long as you're rewarded promptly.

Identifying Your Talents

Your talents help define who you are. Talents include capabilities, aptitudes or skills in virtually any area of human endeavour from athleticism to zoo keeping! People seem to be either born with particular talents or at least to show them at a very young age.

If you're talented at something you make it look easy, because doing something you're talented at requires little willpower or mental effort. Nurturing and developing a talent for, say, music, cooking or swimming makes more sense than choosing to learn a foreign language in the knowledge that you were never very good at languages at school. The mental effort involved in learning something new requires more willpower. However, while it may be easier – that is, it may require less willpower – to pursue something for which you have innate talent or something you're already skilled at, you may want to avoid becoming a one-trick pony and sign up for a cookery course or vocational sessions in art appreciation.

Expanding your talents

Consolidating or building your strengths or talents is generally easier than learning something new. That said, you do well to consider the benefits of familiarity with the benefits of diversity. Because trying something entirely new, such as learning a foreign language, can be mentally taxing is an excellent reason to do precisely that!

Keep in mind that your willpower is a limited resource. If you're taking on a novel challenge, plan it so that it doesn't interfere with other pursuits that rely heavily on willpower.

Broadening and building your talents and strengths requires less willpower than compensating for apparent weaknesses does. You can use your strengths to bolster and conserve your willpower. In a typical day, or portion of a day, aim to intersperse activities that reflect your talents or preferences with those that you find more challenging or boring. For example, if you're outgoing and enjoy social interaction at work, but fall asleep at your desk if you have to do administrative tasks, try to alternate activities so that you spend an hour on the latter followed by an hour meeting customers or colleagues.

Going with your strengths

For years, I felt frustrated about my lack of DIY skills for completing maintenance and repairs at home, and somewhat inadequate. I bought toolkits and manuals (unfortunately, it didn't occur to me to look for a *For Dummies* guide!), but I rarely managed to complete even small projects. Eventually, I decided to do extra contractual professional work on the occasional evening or weekend and use the fees earned to pay skilled tradespeople to maintain my house. In this case, it seemed better for me to utilise the talent I have as a psychologist rather than embark on a steep and possibly hazardous learning curve involving the use of power tools!

Reinforcing your effort

Think of an activity, pastime or hobby that you spend a lot of time or effort doing. The key word here is *effort,* so lying in bed or watching television aren't eligible activities! Examples include gardening, volunteering to help others, concocting innovative recipes in the kitchen, social networking, Tweeting or blogging.

Even though you're choosing freely to invest time and effort in your chosen pursuit, you're still demonstrating personal strengths or resilience. The examples in Table 8-3 illustrate how you can utilise talents. In the right-hand column I speculate on how you can use a component of the talents in a broader context. In Table 8-4 you can have a go yourself.

Table 8-3	Identifying Strengths and Their Applications	
Activity	*Talent Displayed*	*Strategic Use of Talent or Strength*
Tweeting	Being concise, humorous, topical	Communicating well at work; keeping people engaged
Volunteering	Being caring, people-orientated, compassionate; working as part of a team	Using emotional intelligence; having a greater understanding of people's needs; working as part of a team

(continued)

Table 8-3 *(continued)*

Activity	Talent Displayed	Strategic Use of Talent or Strength
Gardening	Stamina; awareness of nature; creativity; ability to plan a year or more in advance	Sustaining effort; thinking creatively; planning projects effectively

Table 8-4   Identifying and Using My Hidden Talents

Activity	Talent	Strategic Use of Talent or Strength

Using Rewarding Activities to Boost Willpower

When you were a child, did your mother or father ever tell you that you could play football or watch television, but first you had to tidy your room or finish your homework? Or do you make these kinds of deals with your own kids? In this scenario, neither the parent or child is likely to have recognised one of the cornerstones of behaviour therapy known as the *Premack Principle*.

The Premack Principle states that a more frequent, and presumably more preferred, behaviour can be used as an incentive to reinforce a less frequent and presumably less preferred behaviour. Enabling access to a favourite computer game or television programme can be used to reinforce (increase the frequency of) a less preferred behaviour such as studying, working late or resisting temptation.

By using the Premack Principle, you have a powerful means of sustaining effort in the longer term. It's also remarkably light on the demands it places on your willpower. You're doing something you love doing!

Pinpointing preferential activities

Your list of rewarding activities is likely to overlap with your strengths and talents. Here, however, I want to encourage you to think of activities that you find pleasurable.

When it comes to pleasure, less is more. Or, to be more precise, less frequent indulgence leads to a more intense experience of pleasure. This isn't meant as a moral judgement but as a reflection on how your brain devalues the pleasure of repeated rewards. I call this *the law of diminishing pleasurable returns*. Nothing quite matches the pleasure of the first sip, or the first bite of the cherry or perhaps the first kiss. That doesn't mean you shouldn't seek out pleasurable experiences. It means that you should spread your pleasure-seeking over time and savour the moment when it arrives.

Going with the flow

The experience of flow isn't confined to any particular activity: it can entail carrying out a skilled or complex piece of work, playing chess, or just getting lost in a fascinating novel. It can be a religious or spiritual experience. Identifying and increasing your experience of flow is important for a general reason and a specific reason, both connected with willpower:

- Generally, people who can generate more flow experiences benefit from a greater sense of well-being and are less prone to depression and other negative emotions.

- Specifically, the experience of flow is a powerful way to reinforce effort, the theme of this chapter. You can reward yourself by creating the opportunity to experience the joy of flow.

Psychologists have identified the following ingredients that combine to generate the experience of flow, although this is inevitably greater than the sum of its parts:

- The pursuit or task requires skill and is a challenge.

- You need to concentrate hard.

- You have a clear goal.

- You get immediate feedback.

- Your involvement feels effortless.

- You have a sense of control.

- You lose track of time, or time appears to stand still.

When you've worked hard on something that challenges and depletes your willpower, suppressed appetites and desires can come to the fore. Thoughts such as 'I deserve a drink/smoke/extra portion/day off work' can sound plausible, in effect giving you permission to indulge yourself. These are the wrong rewards at the wrong time! The message of this chapter is that choosing alternative, more life-enhancing rewards drains unhealthy or unwanted habits of their reinforcement value. If your aim is to lose weight and get fit, a cigarette is *not* a suitable reward! Because your willpower is a limited resource, however, striving for one goal means that you may take your eye off the ball: if your willpower is depleted due to sustained effort or stress, a habit you thought you'd conquered can reassert itself. (Chapter 5 deals with the old adage, 'old habits die hard'.)

Identifying flow experiences

Flow is being immersed or engrossed in an activity or experience for a period of time. Sports commentators describe athletes as being 'in the zone' when they're performing at a consistently high level for a period of time. Another way to say it is that they're 'in the flow'.

Flow experiences reflect your values, motives, strengths and talents. Episodes of flow can induce an authentic natural high that can be life-affirming and promote willpower.

Infrequent or impeded access to flow experiences can lead to negative emotions, including sadness or even depression, and thus weaken your willpower. Identifying activities or pursuits that can deliver the experience of flow is a great way to discover how to reward your efforts.

Amazingly, while going with the flow may require considerable physical and mental energy, it requires very little willpower. The image that's just popped into my mind is of a dog being let off the leash in a large field and just running in sheer exuberant joy with apparently boundless energy. Okay, we humans are a bit more complicated, but have another look at the ingredients of a flow experience. Now, recall a time when you experienced the joy of flow.

Behaviour that's not rewarded fades away. Imagine, for example, getting into a taxi and asking about the driver's day. If you get no response, my guess is that you may try, at most, one more time, but if you're met with further silence you'll read your newspaper or fiddle with your smartphone.

When deploying your willpower to achieve long-term change, it's essential to reward your efforts along the way. Psychologists call this *shaping* behaviour, a bit like coaching or cheerleading you in your quest for the ultimate goal.

Celebrating Success

Often, people run out of willpower before they achieve the goal they set themselves. This chapter focuses primarily on how to overcome this tendency. The most important thing to remember is to reward yourself at each step of the way. Identifying ways to do this is essential for long-term change.

It's vital to savour and celebrate meeting your interim goals, for two reasons:

✔ A typical challenge to your willpower isn't like climbing Mount Everest, planting a flag and going back down again (although you may think that's easier than quitting smoking or losing weight!). The mountaineers can return to their families, write a book and appear on television chat shows. You, however, have to stay on the willpower mountain! There's no point, after all, quitting smoking for a week, and a healthy diet is for life, not just for the summer holidays. So, in order to stay on the summit you need to celebrate and savour the success.

✔ There's always another mountain to climb! Acknowledging, sharing and elaborating on your success boosts your confidence and therefore your willpower for further challenges.

Giving yourself a medal!

Often, being successful is a lonely business because the challenges to be overcome are purely personal. Don't be afraid to congratulate yourself on your success: you're just being balanced and fair to yourself. Like many people, you're probably very quick to identify your mistakes and shortcomings, saying things like, 'I'm useless' or 'I'm stupid.' When you achieve success, make a point of acknowledging how hard you worked and how resourceful you were. Tell your friends and family and spread the word on Twitter and Facebook.

Plan how to celebrate, savour and share your success with friends and family or loved ones. Sharing your success has two important benefits:

✔ Despite the well-intentioned advice and guidance in this chapter, your internal coach may not show up one day, and the alternative rewards you find may be lacklustre. A thoughtful or caring friend can step in with support and encouragement at the critical moment, but you need to confide about your goal so your friends know to offer encouragement.

✔ Engaging significant others in your quest for willpower-driven change can be an excuse for a celebration when the time comes. The inevitable picture on Facebook doesn't need to be a selfie!

Savouring success

Why do people take pictures of graduation ceremonies, weddings and achievements? They do this in order to consolidate the memory and reminisce in the weeks, months and years to come. Although some of these examples reflect excellent use of willpower, in many cases success attributed to willpower is a bit more personal. Maintaining your goal of weight reduction, smoking abstinence or physical fitness is more of a 'one day at a time' process than, say, a once-in-a-lifetime event such as a wedding party or graduation ceremony. Nonetheless, you can create mental souvenirs or memories.

Savouring success anniversaries that can be measured in days, weeks, months or years is another way to consolidate success, build your confidence and prepare for your willpower challenges ahead.

Chapter 9

Maintaining Your Progress

In This Chapter

▶ Using willpower to achieve long-term change

▶ Sustaining willpower with your memory

▶ Motivating your willpower

▶ Harnessing your expectations to improve your willpower

---

*M*ark Twain famously announced, 'Quitting smoking is easy. I've done it a thousand times.' This could be applied to any resolution that requires willpower, whether it be to eat more healthily, to exercise more regularly or to save money. Surveys show, for example, that by mid February 60 per cent of gym membership cards acquired to support a New Year's resolution remain buried in that purse or wallet while those new trainers gather dust in the cupboard. Why does willpower vanish?

In this chapter, I share ways to maintain your willpower in the long term and help you realise that if your approach to maintaining progress is based too much on suppressing impulses, urges and cravings, you'll run out of willpower sooner rather than later. When you're aiming for long-term change, you need to work clever rather than work hard – although effort is always needed at crucial points.

In Chapter 2, I describe the moment-by-moment type of recall and focus as *working memory*. In this chapter, I explore another type of recall and learning: long-term memory.

 Sustainable effort is the key, and this means making positive changes to fill any gap that arises. For example, if you forego your usual mid-morning chocolate bar, sitting morosely at your desk is more likely to undermine your resolve than if you decide to step out for five minutes in the park. Willpower, like nature, abhors a vacuum.

Meeting Your Brain's CEO

Your brain has as many as 200 billion nerve cells, or *neurons,* each with thousands of connections to neighbouring neurons. Your brain evolved to this level of complexity because it has a big job to do: it regulates all your bodily and mental functions. In this regard, willpower equals brain power. One part of the more recently evolved brain system's neocortex, the prefrontal cortex, acts a bit like the chief executive officer (CEO) of a large, complex organisation.

Running hot and cold

Your *prefrontal cortex* is a cool, reflective system that takes responsibility for setting long-term goals, monitoring your progress and preventing you from becoming distracted in the pursuit of these goals.

The evolution of willpower

Willpower evolved in humans in order for them to overcome temptation and achieve long-term goals. Our ancestors learned that it was sometimes better to wait in turn for food, even when hungry, or to forego the opportunity for sex if a large, sexually aroused and hungry male was lurking around. Fashioning a tool, planting a seed or making a fishing net, all tasks our ancestors accomplished, required thinking in the long term. This need to project ahead in time, prioritising long-term benefits over short-term rewards, sculpted the evolution of a newer brain system known as the *neocortex,* or new brain.

The neocortex is what most differentiates human from other mammals, even primates, our closest evolutionary relations. Clever apes can carry out complex, purposeful behaviour and even use simple tools. They can't show the same impulse control we do – chimps don't go on a diet or become celibate for religious reasons – and they can't plan ahead like humans do. They don't plant crops and wait months for food. That is because apes don't have willpower.

Losing grey matter and willpower

Phineas Gage was a competent and trusted 25-year-old employed in building the railway in Vermont, USA. This wasn't easy work, and it was necessary to use explosives to blast through rock. On September 13, 1848, the explosives detonated prematurely. A metal rod used for compacting the explosives, measuring over a metre in length and weighing over 6 kilograms, smashed through Phineas Gage's left cheek and exited through the top right side of his head. Remarkably, he regained consciousness quickly and sat upright as he was taken by cart to see the local doctor in Cavendish, Vermont.

He soon returned to work, and apparently showed no loss of intelligence, motor control or language. But he'd changed. Friends, family and workmates noticed he'd become unreliable, irresponsible and offensive, frequently swearing and disregarding social conventions. This wasn't the Gage from before the accident. He lost his job as a railway foreman and apparently drifted from job to job, eventually living in San Francisco, California. People reported that he began to drink and gamble excessively. He died in 1860, aged just 36, probably from epilepsy linked to his brain injuries.

Although the circumstances are still debated, this anecdote shows that self-control or willpower is distinct from intelligence, knowledge or skills, and requires an intact and fully functioning brain.

The distraction comes, directly or indirectly, from the other major brain system: the hot, impulsive brain nestling beneath the cerebral cortex. This includes the limbic system, where emotions, appetites and desires are triggered. If the hot system had a slogan it would be, 'I want gratification, and I want it now!' In direct contrast, the cool system looks to the future with rules like, 'It would be lovely now, but it's better if I wait, because I have other priorities.' The story in the nearby sidebar, 'Losing grey matter and willpower', provides a stark account of what can happen when the prefrontal cortex is damaged.

In order to function effectively, you need for both your hot and emotional and your cool and rational systems to operate in harmony. Without the former you'd be like *Star Trek's* Mr Spock, lacking in emotion and probably motivation – as well as friends! Looking at the other extreme, I leave it to your imagination to figure out what you'd be like if you succumbed to all your impulses all the time! Of course, these are extreme scenarios; mostly the CEO has to make more subtle decisions – for example, 'Is the decision to work on the project for another hour and skip the cold beer?' or 'Shall I spend another 20 minutes on the exercise machine or shall I grab a pizza and go home?'

Putting your willpower CEO to work

The best way to exploit your willpower in order to achieve long-term change is by using your brain's CEO, or prefrontal cortex. If your CEO had a name it would be – you probably guessed it – Will Power (a female Willow or Wilhelmina, or a male William)! The CEO has access to thinking and planning tools such as problem-solving skills. Will is especially concerned with reining in the hot, impulsive brain. This requires considerable mental energy, but is by no means the only challenge confronting Will. No business can survive without being active in pursuit of its corporate goals, and the CEO of your brain also has to keep scanning the horizon and planning the long journey ahead. This effort can lead to the hard-pressed Will becoming exhausted.

Exhaustion is one of the most common reasons for willpower lapses and fades. As an overloaded, tired or distracted CEO switches off, the hot and impulsive brain temporarily seizes control. When this happens, as sooner or later it does, old habits return and impulses are given free rein.

At CEO Will Power's disposal are three powerful weapons – thinking tools – to prevent Will Power being overwhelmed, and to limit the negative consequences and resume the task in hand:

✔ Prioritising or focusing attention

✔ Monitoring and updating progress

✔ Overcoming temptation and controlling impulses

Ongoing tasks you can undertake to help your willpower CEO stay strong include:

✔ Keeping fit with aerobic exercise

✔ Managing your stress and doing relaxation exercises

✔ Making and keeping social engagements

✔ Keeping yourself mentally stimulated

✔ Taking omega-3 supplements

Table 9-1 outlines how each thinking tool can be deployed and enhanced.

Table 9-1   Boosting Willpower With Thinking Tools

Thinking Tool	Sample Action	Way To Improve It
Focus	Think of long-term benefits. For example: I'll get a good grade; I'll become healthier; I'll look good in a bikini (not the author!).	Meditate; read novels; do brain-training exercises; take predictable and regular breaks from concentrating; switch off your phone for an evening.
Updating Progress or Monitoring Challenges	Keep a diary; subscribe to email or smartphone alerts.	Rehearse your goal frequently; anticipate challenges and how to cope with them ('*If* I'm tempted, *then* I'll . . . ').
Controlling Impulses (or 'Get out of my office!')	Say no to a cigarette when you want one; ignore the '50% off' sale sign at the shoe shop.	Practise small acts of self-denial; avoid sugary foods such as cakes and choose foods that release glucose slowly – pulses, most fruits or wholemeal bread.

The good news is that your CEO becomes more skilled, because your brain constantly reorganises or rewires itself as you encounter new events and situations. As you read this paragraph, new connections are being formed in your brain! This process, known as *neuroplasticity,* or 'what fires together, wires together', slows down as you get older but doesn't stop at any age. New brain cells (known as neurons) can also be created, a process known as *neurogenesis.* These two processes, involving rewiring and repairing your brain, are crucial to fostering willpower.

Nurturing your brain – striving for what's known as 'neural fitness' – is like giving your CEO a good diet, sufficient time to rest and recover, but also new challenges to keep in tip-top condition.

Taxi drivers versus bus drivers

When researchers used neuroimaging to study the brains of London taxi drivers, who are required to memorise thousands of routes throughout the metropolis, they discovered that the regions of the drivers' brains involved in memory were significantly larger than those of a carefully selected control group. The control group were London bus drivers, who need to memorise perhaps one or two routes for months or even years.

Consider how much easier it was for the cabbies to conserve their willpower (presumably in order to tell their passengers where the Government is going wrong!) with the aid of such a powerful and flexible memory system.

For the most part, if you're just chilling out and not relying too much on your willpower, having a poorly maintained brain (or inefficient CEO) doesn't trouble you. However, if you're using willpower to take on challenges, you may discover that your ability to remain focused and determined is lacking. Training your willpower can prepare you for these challenges over the long term. The good news is your brain can rewire itself and you can learn to think and behave differently. The less good news is that the circuits in your brain concerned with reward and pleasure have long memories. These can't easily be erased, but they can be modified and overwritten, as I explain in the next section.

Using Your Memory to Boost Your Willpower

You probably think your memory is a bit like a digital video recorder, diligently creating accurate records of your life and times. It isn't! Especially when you're not paying attention, your memory can be wildly inaccurate. If you miss something, your memory can do its best to guess what it was. For example, if you're presented with a list of words such as 'table', 'dinner', 'knife', 'plate', 'cooker' and 'kitchen', you're subsequently more likely to falsely agree that the words 'food' or 'hungry' were in the list. This is because your memory loves to chunk or categorise information, because most of the time it helps recall.

Despite its honest mistakes, your memory can help you stay focused on your goals. Keeping your goal uppermost in your mind is the single most helpful thing your memory does to boost your willpower.

Exploring memory

You have three types of memory:

- **Memory for doing:** Often called *muscle memory* or *procedural memory,* this type of memory helps you recall skills you've acquired, such as riding a bicycle, playing a musical instrument or participating in a sport.

- **Memory for recounting:** This type of memory, also known as *episodic memory,* enables you to describe your first day in a new job or your last holiday.

- **Memory for knowing:** Knowing that Paris is the capital of France or that a high-interest-rate loan costs more than a low-interest one are the types of facts and general knowledge your memory holds.

These three types of memory are some of your greatest assets in translating short-term change into long-term progress. Your memory functions help you get the most from your willpower in these ways:

- Recalling occasions when your willpower worked for you and when it didn't. (I talk more about this in Chapter 6.) This is your library of coping tools, with a few warning signs thrown in.

- Recalling why you decided to harness your willpower to aim for change. Yes, you can forget what it felt like to be overweight, hung over or overdrawn. Sometimes your memory needs to give you a friendly reminder.

Burying your old memories with new ones

A question that featured on my undergraduate exam papers (ironically, the only one I can remember a few decades later!) was 'Elephants never forget; do people?' I must confess to ignorance with regard to the elephant's apparently legendary memory, but humans can retain and recall a vast amount throughout life. We do, however, forget, but this is more down to problems with access or retrieval rather than loss of the original memory.

What is clear is that memories associated with pleasure, fear or other intense emotions are enduring. They can, however, be overwritten or covered over by newer memories. If you've been in a terrifying car crash, you gradually become more relaxed on car journeys, but if you have to brake sharply and swerve, the memories of the crash come flooding back. Memories for pleasure, what I call *appetitive memories,* have similar potency. Understanding and managing good memories is a core skill in using willpower to achieve lasting change.

Developing new memories

Don't throw the baby out with the bathwater! If you decide that you no longer want to drop into your local bar on the way home from work, or you decide to skip your regular visits to the Italian restaurant on the corner, because you want to cut down on your drinking, you can think of other ways of maintaining your social network. Consider:

- Joining a club or neighbourhood society
- Inviting friends around at the weekend
- Organising a night out at the theatre
- Cajoling a few friends to go on a bike ride on Sunday afternoon (step 1: get yourself a bicycle!)
- Or, consider still going to the trattoria, but sticking to a bottle of sparkling water

Your expectations of how you will feel influence how you actually feel. See the nearby sidebar 'John's leather jacket' and the section 'Expecting Your Willpower to Work', later in this chapter.

Going back to favourite activities

Your brain loves the familiar or the routine. If you enjoyed doing something once, you're likely to enjoy doing it again. The phrase 'It's like riding a bicycle' is apt. This is not *just* about cycling; it tells you that you have a long memory for anything you were once good at doing, whether it's karaoke singing or knitting (although not at the same time!)

John's leather jacket

My friend John recently passed away. At the funeral reception, his tearful widow told me that he wanted me to have his favourite leather jacket. He'd worn this expensive item only once or twice, because he was keeping it for very special occasions. On a sad day, this made me feel even sadder. John rarely had the chance to enjoy wearing his jacket, and now it was too late.

Sometimes, willpower can be too strict, and you should gratify yourself in the moment. You may not get the chance again. You also need to reward yourself with the occasional indulgence. Whenever I hesitate about doing something new or rewarding, I remember the leather jacket and usually go for it.

Think of the habit or unwanted behaviour you're aiming to change. It may be an unhealthy diet, too little exercise or too much time spent gaming or on social networking sites. Now, try to recall how you passed the time before this became problematic or excessive. Did you enjoy travel, reading, going to the theatre, gardening, fishing or exploring the great outdoors? Make a plan to pick up that old pastime.

Realising the willpower-memory bonus

Favourite activities are willpower-light, meaning they don't take much willpower to complete. Unless you're trying to establish a new world record or train for a marathon, sports, hobbies or other recreational pursuits don't compete too hard for willpower. On the contrary, doing familiar physical activities can contribute to boosting your willpower in some or all of the following ways:

✔ Being physically active increases your brain fitness by making brain cells more communicative.

✔ Recreational activities broaden and build your social network. They give your brain a workout and boost your willpower capacity. For example, you can become a member of a sports team, contribute to running a book club, or organise the gardening group's annual general meeting. If you're retired, or are about to retire, pastimes especially important, because staying active keeps you mentally sharp.

✔ You sleep better and have a more regulated appetite when you're physically active and/or mentally engaged. Your willpower gets a boost, too.

✔ You have to switch off your mobile and be out of range for emails! The intermittent and relentless stream of messages you receive drains your willpower: the decision to ignore, respond to or delete an email taps into the willpower engine – your working memory.

Predictable time off

Why do air-traffic controllers take frequent breaks? Obviously, because their ability to sustain attention – a core aspect of willpower – diminishes over time. Even after 15 minutes of concentration, you can begin to make mistakes such as missing or misinterpreting something someone said at a meeting. Reassuringly, air-traffic controllers are adept at staying focused (and systems ensure that any slips are detected and corrected), but nobody can stay vigilant for extended periods. After an hour of intense concentration, error rates increase significantly. This is a failure of willpower, because willpower is a limited resource.

Monitoring your phone or computer for messages or alerts is nothing like as taxing as controlling aircraft carrying hundreds of passengers, but it also draws on a limited source of willpower. Recall, for example, having a conversation with your passengers when driving. As soon as you approach a busy junction, the conversation dries up as you focus on the road and your passengers shut up!

Researchers in Boston, USA, encouraged consultants to switch off their phones and email systems for an agreed number of hours at the same time each week. This blackout needed to be agreed with team colleagues, because they were expected to avoid emailing or calling during this period. The benefits of a respite from the always-connected world fade if you're assailed by a flurry of emails, texts and voicemails when you repower your smartphone! But benefits did result from this trial, as measured by increased job satisfaction, contentment and work–life balance.

Why not try this every week? Start by deciding that checking your emails when you arrive home from work can stop, or get a separate phone for personal or non-work use. That's what I did, and it works for me.

Using Motivation to Boost Willpower

Motivation can compensate for depleted willpower. Whether your goal is losing weight, getting fit or finishing a project on time, reminding yourself of the reasons you committed to your goal in the first instance can recharge your motivational battery and jump-start your willpower. Your willpower needs this motivational power, especially when running on empty.

The equation is:

$$\text{Willpower} \times \text{Motivation} \times \text{Ability} = \text{Level of Success}$$

High levels of motivation can compensate for low levels of willpower. Imagine, for example, it's Sunday afternoon and you're struggling to assign time to finishing a work project. You'd rather do (almost) anything else. But you know that the project has to be ready for the 9:00 a.m. meeting the next day. Assuming you have the competency to accomplish your chosen goal (if not, it could be a bit late to develop at this point!), you can increase the likelihood of a successful outcome by refocusing on your motivation. Ask yourself these questions:

- ✔ Why did I volunteer to do the project? Reasons may include the skills you might acquire or the new working relationships and friendships that may ensue.

- ✔ What are the short-term and long-term benefits to the final customers or service users? These can mirror your own motives and values. This focus makes it less likely that you'll be distracted by the lure of the game on TV or a desire to just chill for the afternoon.

- ✔ What are the long-term benefits to my role and my career? Asking this helps you overcome the desire to have a smaller, sooner reward – which may be simply not having to make an effort on a Sunday afternoon – instead of the larger, later reward promised by your efforts.

Focusing on long-term or delayed benefits resulting from exerting willpower is a powerful motivational tool. Willpower enables you to look over the horizon, into the long-term future. Forgoing short-term rewards such as the benefit of a relaxing Sunday afternoon or the indulgence of a sugar-laden dessert can be challenging, but maintaining focus on the long-term benefits can help you overcome the tyranny of 'I want it now'.

The (bi)cycle of change

One of my clients in the psychology clinic where I work, I'll call him Giles, struggled for years to quit drinking. Last December, after a bout of particularly heavy drinking, he resolved to quit. Following what proved to be a false start, lasting just ten days, he came up with the right approach. Giles had always been a keen cyclist, but over the years had cycled less and stayed at home drinking more and more often. His goal was to buy an expensive bicycle and go on a cycling holiday in Wales (he was also planning to buy some waterproofs!).

He calculated that he was spending on average £12 a day on the wine and beer that he took home to drink. He created a spreadsheet on his computer, and around the time he'd normally go to the off licence he typed in £12 on the spreadsheet. He estimated that after three months or so, he'd have sufficient funds to buy the bicycle he'd selected.

Note that he didn't use real money. He just worked out how much he was saving and what he could do with those funds. This provided both an incentive and a reminder on a daily basis. The goal was also in keeping with his preferences – he'd always loved cycling and travel – and the high value he placed on keeping fit.

You can probably think of something from your personal preferences – perhaps something you've lost touch with – that's also in keeping with your values. Rediscovering this could bolster your willpower, because *doing* something is generally less demanding on willpower than concentrating on *not* doing something.

Expecting Your Willpower to Work

What you expect to happen has a big influence on what you subsequently experience. When you swallow a painkiller, you can feel relief before the drug can do its job or when it's barely in your bloodstream. When anxious people swallow a pill to calm themselves down, they begin to feel more relaxed before the drug attaches to the inhibitory receptors that dampen down the brain's activities. People experience relief from pain and anxiety even when given a dummy pill. This is known as the *placebo effect.*

A *placebo* (from the Latin word meaning 'to please') reflects what people *expect* to happen when they believe they've taken a pill, a drink or something they expect to deliver a specific outcome.

Researchers tested the validity of the placebo effect by recruiting participants who were given either an alcoholic drink or a non-alcoholic drink. Half of each group were misled (lied to, but in the interests of scientific enquiry), so some participants believed they were drinking alcohol when they weren't, and some in fact drank non-alcoholic drinks when they believed they had alcohol in their glasses. Table 9-2 shows the results for the four groups.

Table 9-2 Expectation Influences Experience		
	Given Alcohol	*Not Given Alcohol*
Told They Were Drinking Alcohol	Acted intoxicated	Acted intoxicated
Told They Weren't Drinking Alcohol	Acted sober	Acted sober

What the person *believed* or expected to be in the glass influenced the response more than the effects of the alcohol did. Participants who believed they'd been given alcohol were likely to report heightened feelings of sociability, sexual arousal or even aggression whether they'd been given alcohol or simply told they had.

Similarly, in participants who were given alcohol but didn't believe this was the case, the effects of the alcohol weren't apparent.

This experiment demonstrates that beliefs and expectations can have a big impact on how you react or feel. Applied to willpower, this means that often your impulses are driven by what you expect to happen rather than what subsequently happens.

If you anticipate a pleasurable event, your brain's reward centre gets fired up ahead of time. It's like not having your cake but feeling as if you're eating it!

However, when an expected reward doesn't arrive, disappointed and disgruntled dopamine receptors – the brain's reward cells – abound. That's difficult to change, so the best technique is to challenge the expectation. Knowing, for example, that it's what you believe to be in your glass, rather than what is in your glass, that influences your mood challenges the expectation that you need to drink alcohol to get into a party mood.

Similarly, if you tend to reach for a pill at the first twinge of pain, hint of anxiety or delay in getting to sleep, try to challenge the expectation. Willpower is better than pill power in the long term.

Part III
Following Up for Success

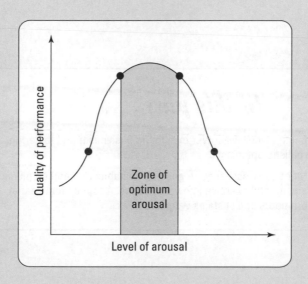

Find out more about willpower at www.dummies.com/
extras/willpower.

In this part . . .

✔ Engage your willpower by fighting pessimism and fostering realistic optimism.

✔ Manage stress, acquire good sleep habits and embed physical and mental exercise into your routine. Adopt a lifestyle that promotes and sustains willpower.

Chapter 10

Developing and Maintaining Realistic Optimism

··

In This Chapter

▶ Being a realistic optimist

▶ Fighting procrastination and perfectionism

▶ Recognising that pessimists and optimists think differently

▶ Increasing your self-confidence and your willpower

··

*W*hether you're an optimist or a pessimist affects your ability to engage your willpower:

✓ An optimist anticipates or predicts the best possible outcome.

✓ A pessimist anticipates or predicts the worst possible outcome.

If you're optimistic, you're likely to persevere in pursuing your goal or objective. In other words, you're likely to use your willpower. If, on the other hand, you tend towards a pessimistic outlook, you're less likely to show sustained effort and likely to become demoralised by failures and setbacks. Why, after all, should you invest willpower striving for a goal that you believe you have little chance of realising?

In this chapter, I show you how to be a realistic optimist who anticipates gaining the best possible outcome when using will-power to achieve personal goals. Note that this isn't intended as a platitude along the lines of 'always hope for the best'. Neither does it indemnify you against failures and setbacks. Fostering realistic optimism does, however, ensure that you use willpower to initiate and sustain your best effort to achieve your goals.

Aiming for Realistic Optimism

In the context of promoting willpower, optimism is about *realistic* predictions about how things will unfold. Feeling certain that you'll win the lottery – a chance of about 1 in 14 million in the UK – has less to do with optimism and more to do with hope, if not desperation! Pursuing a goal that's attainable and realistic is more likely to be facilitated by realistic optimism and jeopardised by a pessimistic mindset. If you're optimistic, you're more likely to set a personally meaningful goal that challenges you in the first place, and you're more likely to persevere in the face of difficulty.

Realistic optimism also entails making sense of setbacks, and indeed learning from them. In this regard, this chapter shares a similar theme to that of Chapter 7, in which I suggest a compassionate, non-blaming response to failure. In this chapter, self-blame is again highlighted but in a different way. For instance, if you tend to shoulder the blame when things go wrong, the suggestion is that you are the problem. Accordingly, should the situation recur in the future, you'll be the problem again. Repeatedly blaming or attacking yourself when things go wrong can lead to you developing a mindset that psychologists call *learned helplessness,* surely the complete opposite of willpower. It's therefore important for you to identify the thinking patterns associated with pessimism so that you can replace them with a more optimistic but balanced way of interpreting your successes and failures.

Another form of unrealistic optimism is the 'it'll never happen to me' attitude. An example of this outlook is seen in the pack-a-day smokers who believe themselves somehow immune from the hazards of smoking, perhaps citing the longevity of an elderly aunt who smoked 40 cigarettes a day until she turned 100. She was indeed fortunate to live that long, because smoking knocks about ten years off the average lifespan.

An optimistic outlook helps sustain your effort in the face of the inevitable setbacks that occur when you're engaged in challenges that draw on your willpower. Optimists have setbacks, but recover; pessimists are more likely to just quit, most likely because they unfairly blame themselves.

Determining what makes an optimist or a pessimist

Three broad factors help determine the degree to which you're likely to be relatively more optimistic or pessimistic:

- **Genetic make-up,** expressed as personality characteristics. For instance, pessimists are likely to be emotionally sensitive and less open to new experiences, whereas optimists are more likely to seek out novel experiences and tend to score high on the personality factor termed *conscientiousness*. (Check out the section on the Big Five personality factors in Chapter 2 for more about personality.)

- **Life experiences,** especially those that occur through the developmental periods of childhood and adolescence. Repeated experience of difficult or seemingly uncontrollable life events steers people towards pessimism.

- **Emotional support** by those close to you. Exposure to adversity or feeling not in control during your childhood, or indeed at any stage in life, doesn't necessarily engender a sense of pessimism. However, if you weren't given love, support and understanding in times of need by those close to you, a negative or pessimistic interpretation of events is likely to ensue.

The combination of a particular type of personality, exposure to adversity in childhood, and emotionally distant or critical parents may contribute to a pessimistic outlook on life. In my experience, however, these three factors don't usually coincide; they're invariably balanced by positive or protective factors such as the love and understanding of a friend or sibling, or the support and guidance of an inspiring teacher.

You don't choose your parents (and of course the genetic legacy they donate to you), and you can't erase difficult or painful events from your past. You can, however, learn to think differently about your past and to envisage a more positive future, which gives you more scope to utilise your willpower.

Appreciating the good with the not so good

If you're tempted to bemoan the fact that you're emotionally sensitive or not especially conscientious, consider the other side of the personality coin. For example, if you're emotionally sensitive and prone to anxiety or worry, this may make you empathic, caring and understanding. You can also have too much of an apparently good thing such as conscientiousness, which can, when taken to extremes, result in rigidly sticking to plans or becoming obsessed with detail.

If you never experienced any setbacks or problems growing up, imagine how disconcerting you'd find it the first time you experienced a real challenge!

Perfectionism and Procrastination: The Twin Enemies of Willpower!

Without doubt, from the perspective of willpower, the most challenging personality characteristic is perfectionism. Continually striving for unrealistically high standards and beating yourself up when you fail – the defining features of perfectionism – can combine to drain your willpower. Perfectionism's weapon of choice is procrastination or simply avoiding doing things in a timely fashion.

I've been planning to write this section of the book for several weeks, but I kept putting it off! When I finally wrote a few paragraphs, I wasn't satisfied with the result, and another few weeks elapsed. Recognise anything familiar here? I was, of course, experiencing the two biggest barriers to human progress: *procrastination,* postponing doing something – 'the thief of time' according to Charles Dickens – and *perfectionism,* the unrealistic expectation that anything less than 100 per cent represents failure. Both excessive delay and setting unrealistic or unattainable standards can deplete your willpower in different ways.

In combination, perfectionism and procrastination amount to 'won't power' – surely the opposite of willpower.

Recognising procrastination

Procrastination is a suitably long word to describe what's often a long delay between realising that something needs to be done and actually doing it. For example, you may think, 'This essay is too difficult for me, I haven't done enough background reading' and further delay writing the essay. Or you may think, 'The dentist may criticise me for not keeping regular appointments' and put off making an appointment. Your excuses for putting things off may be apparently plausible, but they're also biased or simply guesses that may prove wrong.

Engaging in perfectionism

Perfectionism shouldn't be confused with valuing and striving for perfection. Aiming for perfection is a good thing and an excellent use of willpower! *Perfectionism,* on the other hand, has three key features that in fact reduce the likelihood of achieving valued goals and fritter away your willpower:

- If you're behaving as a perfectionist, you're more likely to set unrealistic goals or aspire to unattainable standards. This makes it more likely that you'll give up or throw in the towel from a willpower perspective!

  For example, a perfectionist is more likely to become disheartened when learning something new, because it takes considerable practice to achieve the high level of competence aspired to. (For some reason, I've just remembered my unsuccessful attempts to learn to windsurf, although I don't regard myself as a perfectionist!)

- Perfectionists base their estimation of self-worth to an excessive degree on their performance or ability, rather than, say, their value to others in the role of parent, partner or mentor. This leads to a tendency for perfectionists to blame themselves when they fail to reach the high standards they set themselves.

- When perfectionists make judgements about their performance, they rely too much on the opinions of others, in particular going out of their way to avoid criticism. Think about it: if you're striving for perfection, criticism is the last thing you want to hear. A perfectionist may think, for example, 'I simply can't tolerate critical comments at work, therefore I can't afford to make mistakes.'

In combination, these factors mean that perfectionists can end up achieving less than people with more realistic standards or those who are less concerned about the possibility of being criticised. In an effort to avoid criticism or failure – the worst things that can happen to a perfectionist – procrastination and avoidance ensue. Perfectionists can therefore become disappointed and demoralised, and be more likely to avoid future challenges such as applying for a job at the upper end of their range of competence.

If you have perfectionist tendencies, you're likely to set unrealistically high standards not just for yourself but for others. This can create tension and conflict, which can deplete your willpower. Even more directly, you may be forced to deploy willpower to suppress your criticism of others.

In his famous book *How to Win Friends and Influence People,* Dale Carnegie points out that nobody likes to be criticised. If you have perfectionist tendencies, you're likely to criticise others. However, you may well need the support of these individuals to fully utilise your willpower. So, if you feel the need to deliver negative feedback, try suggesting something positive such as, 'Have you thought about doing it this way . . . ?' or 'You might find it easier to do it this way.'

Overcoming unhelpful tendencies

Taming your tendencies to procrastinate and display perfectionism gives your willpower a fighting chance. The next sections offer advice on dealing with each.

Fighting procrastination

To deal with tasks you've put off, ask yourself about tasks that have remained on your to-do list for weeks when you could have accomplished them in days, hours or even minutes. Use the following questions and process to move past your procrastination:

1. **Identify the activity or task.**

2. **Focus on the first thought that comes into your mind when you think of it. What feeling or emotion is linked to the thought and the task?**

   You may have thoughts and feelings that undermine how you perceive your capability or motivation; for example, 'I can't do this; it's overwhelming,' or 'This isn't fair. I shouldn't have to do this.' Whatever the thought associated with the particular task or activity, it's helpful to know it.

3. **Ask yourself how true or untrue the thought is and whether it's more likely to prove true or untrue.**

   The best way to re-evaluate your thought is to challenge the assumption that it's true. You can do this by gathering evidence that doesn't support the thought. For example, if you're asked to take on more responsibility at work and you think, 'I won't be able to cope with this,' try reflecting on other occasions when you had to deal with more challenge or responsibility. A more balanced thought could be something like, 'Taking this on at work will be a big challenge, but I've managed to deal with similar demands in the past.'

4. **Look at your diary or think ahead to when you have half an hour free in the next few days, and set a time to address the task.**

   For example, 'At 10 a.m. on Saturday morning, just after breakfast, I'll spend 45 minutes writing the report or essay (or book chapter!). Whether I make hardly any progress or significant progress, I'll stop for a break at 10:45, with the option of continuing if I choose to.

When you finish this exercise, recollect your thoughts. How do they compare to the earlier thoughts you had when you were anticipating the task? My guess is that the reality proves less daunting than the expectation. This reflects one of the most common distortions in human thinking: predicting that things will be worse or more difficult than they subsequently prove to be. This negative emotional forecasting is the enemy of willpower, because it can prevent you from even trying to fulfil your potential.

Recognising your perfectionist moments

Your perfectionist moment may be when you don't get the high grade you expect or think you deserve. It may be when your annual appraisal at work doesn't end with the words 'another brilliant year, demonstrating creativity, productivity and enthusiasm'!

The perfectionist isn't just an individual striving for perfection or excellence. What's not to like about that? Perfectionism is more than just setting high standards: it's a way of interpreting and reacting to events or situations that affected you. Perfectionists base their self-esteem or self-worth entirely or largely on successful performance in a given task. For a perfectionist, a bad day in the workplace or a poor grade in an exam is evidence of personal failure or inadequacy. This direct link between perceived success and how perfectionists value themselves drives the relentless pursuit of ultimately unattainable standards.

When you recall an event, do you look at the whole picture, taking account of the positives, or do you selectively focus on one or two less-than-positive things? Do you fall into the infamous trap of thinking in black and white, in which everything is either complete success or complete failure, with no shades of grey? Thinking that your whole presentation was awful because you forgot to mention one of your key points is black-and-white thinking. Instead, you can focus on the fact that you remembered four of your five key points. If you think of your performance on a sliding scale, you avoid boxing yourself in with judgements that label your performance as either a disaster or a master work.

Using adversity

Imagine for a moment that you grew up in an idyllic situation. Your parents were perfect, and sibling rivalry unheard of. Your pets never died. At school, you were never teased, bullied, picked on by a teacher, or embarrassed in any way. Stretching the imagination, to be sure.

Now, consider a less rosy scenario that may be a bit more realistic. Imagine arriving for your first day at work or university. Most people ignore you and some people are rude to you. Even worse, you're the target of practical jokes aimed to humiliate you. (My elderly neighbour told me that on his first day on a building site,

he was sent to ask the foreman for a bucket of steam and some mysterious objects known as sky hooks!) Next, imagine your actual childhood and upbringing – including the love, friendship, happiness and laughter, but also the disappointments, embarrassments, losses and regrets.

Which scenario do you think prepares you better for the adult world and provides a more realistic context for utilising your willpower? I would bet on the latter, because adversity teaches us valuable lessons, not just about the world but about our strengths and weaknesses.

Staying in the perfectionist mode can be demoralising, demotivating and distracting. Perfectionism is the enemy of willpower. Set out to achieve the optimal outcome, not the perfect outcome.

Set attainable goals and realistic standards, and don't allow yourself to be preoccupied by fear of criticism.

Thinking Styles and Predicting Positive or Negative Outcomes

Optimistic or pessimistic judgements are necessarily predictive. You simply don't know what will happen at the job interview, during the university exam or 14 days into your quit-smoking or fitness programme. That doesn't stop your subconscious speculation!

Predicting the future

Speculation about the future – in effect, guesswork – is based on a set of rules and assumptions you acquire throughout your life. Over time, you develop a set of rules to make sense of what sometimes seems like a relentless cascade of life events. Psychologists call these judgements *attributional,* insofar as they explain or attribute causality to life events and outcomes. In turn, these judgements influence how you make predictions about future events and outcomes, which in turn influences your resolve and commitment to pursuing your goals – your willpower.

Compare the attitudes about going into a job interview of two candidates who have the same qualifications:

- **Pessimistic prediction:** 'On the basis of past experience, it seems unrealistic to expect a job offer at this interview.'

- **Optimistic prediction:** 'I've not had much luck at recent interviews, but I've probably had more experience at interviews than the other candidates have!'

Which mindset do you think is likely to lead to the welcome words, 'You're hired'? My belief is that the more optimistic candidate will show more persistence in aiming to convince the panel to say those words.

Live longer with an optimistic outlook

Almost 60 years after the diaries were written, psychologist Deborah Danner and her colleagues carefully examined the records that 180 young nuns were required to keep when they entered the convent as young women during the 1930s.

The researchers ranked the content of the diaries according to how optimistic they were; for example, 'I look forward [to religious life] with eager joy' compared with less optimistic or more neutral statements such as 'I intend to do my best.'

The nuns who wrote the most positive diaries were found to live an average of ten years longer than those who expressed the least positive emotions.

The striking aspect of this study is that the nuns experienced very similar lifestyles in terms of factors such as occupation (most were teachers), diet and access to health care. This suggests that an optimistic outlook was indeed influential in promoting longevity and, presumably, health.

Exploring thinking styles with the 3Ps

Your brain is programmed to look for causes, particularly when the results of your actions have negative implications. Your brain likes to find a scapegoat, and that scapegoat can be you! Of course, your brain also seeks an explanation when good things happen. So if, after an interview, you're offered the job, your brain tries to assign cause and effect, and you may wonder, 'Did I do well at the job interview because my rivals weren't very good, or was it down to my track record and good performance?'

You can have negative beliefs about or explanations of positive events, as well as positive explanations of negative events. By paying attention to these interpretations you can identify underlying biases that steer you towards an optimistic or a pessimistic outlook. Overall, blaming yourself for negative outcomes can undermine you, but failing to give yourself due credit for success means you lose out in other ways. Combined, both biases can undermine your willpower.

The psychologist Martin Seligman suggests that the process of making sense of why you fail or succeed has three dimensions, known as the *3Ps,* which stand for personal involvement, permanence and pervasiveness.

Personal involvement

Generally, people account for failures by assigning responsibility either to themselves – according to the degree to which they perceive themselves to be personally involved – or to an outside agent. The former is termed *internal focus* and the latter *external focus:*

- ✔ **Internal** or **personal focus** often takes the form of self-blame or self-criticism, revealed by thoughts such as, 'I'm stupid; I'm forgetful,' if you leave home without your keys, for example.

- ✔ **External focus** tends to shift the blame to situational or contextual factors, as in, 'It's such a windy day, the door slammed shut in a second,' or 'My neighbour distracted me just as I was about to pick up my keys.'

For people with a pessimistic outlook, a tendency to blame themselves when things go wrong isn't balanced by a tendency to take due credit when things go well. Instead, in the face of success, the pessimist seems to switch from internal to external explanations. For example, after organising a successful social event, pessimists may say, 'Everybody got on really well together, which turned the party into a really fun event,' and completely overlook their own contribution.

In emotional contexts, for instance if your partner ends your long-term relationship, the degree to which you have an internal focus or an external focus can be crucial in how you cope. Compare 'I was selfish and I didn't put enough into the relationship' with 'My career seemed to become the priority, and my partner needed more love and support than I was able to offer.' The second interpretation acknowledges an external influence without discounting the personal involvement vital to any relationship.

Permanence

A pessimistic-minded person may view any slip-up as evidence of a more lasting or permanent failure. The failure is seen as consistent or stable over time. For example, a pessimist who misses a flight or is late for an important meeting may think, 'I'm stupid; I'm careless.' Note that the perceived failing is seen as evidence of a relatively *permanent* deficiency. An optimist is more likely to see the event as an uncharacteristic mistake – as in, 'That's not like me; I rarely slip up like that.' The optimist shrugs off mistakes without viewing them as evidence of permanent shortcomings.

With regard to good events, the situation is reversed. Pessimists explain success to themselves in terms of temporary causes such as mood or effort – for example, 'I worked hard that day' – whereas optimists go for enduring factors: 'My talent and capability got me the job.'

Pervasiveness

Pessimists tend to over-generalise from a given setback and interpret one slip-up as evidence of more universal failure across a range of situations. After a mistake, a pessimist may say, 'I can't do anything right!' An optimist, on the other hand, is more likely to interpret the problem along more specific lines: 'I can make mistakes when I rush.'

In the face of success, the opposite occurs, with optimists interpreting success as evidence of their intrinsic value or competence, but pessimists thinking they just got lucky.

For example, if a man tells his long-term partner that he wants to end the relationship, and implies that he doesn't find his ex-partner attractive, the woman's pervasive, pessimistic stance is, 'I'm not sexually attractive.' Her more specific response is, 'I'm not attractive to him.'

Summarising the 3Ps

Table 10-1 relates the 3Ps to optimistic and pessimistic ways of making sense of positive and negative events.

Table 10-1 Optimistic and Pessimistic Thinking Styles

3Ps	Optimistic Explanation For:		Pessimistic Explanation For:	
	Positive Events	*Negative Events*	*Positive Events*	*Negative Events*
Personal Involvement	I put in the effort and I deserve the success.	The task was difficult and I wasn't given clear instructions.	The interview questions were easy to answer.	I made several crucial errors.

3Ps	Optimistic Explanation For:		Pessimistic Explanation For:	
	Positive Events	Negative Events	Positive Events	Negative Events
Permanence	I'm talented.	I was exhausted that day.	I made a huge effort on the day and it paid off.	I never quite get it right at interviews.
Pervasiveness	I can be successful at whatever I choose to do.	I don't seem to be good at that particular task.	I'm good at job interviews.	No employer is going to offer a job to someone like me.

Recall a recent personal experience of a setback, making a mistake or receiving disappointing news. This may involve a scenario in which your willpower wasn't up to the challenge. Conjure up as vivid a recall as possible, trying to get back in touch with how you felt in the moment. This can help you retrieve what you were thinking. In turn, this helps you recognise some of the less helpful thoughts and assumptions that demoralise you and sap your willpower. Next, repeat the same exercise, only this time recall a successful experience or achievement in similar detail. Use the 3Ps described in the previous sections.

Linking Self-confidence and Willpower

Pessimistic thinking styles are closely linked to low self-confidence and low self-esteem. Low self-esteem is a generalised type of low self-worth, based on a perception of consistent, cumulative failure or inadequacy.

Low self-confidence and low self-esteem lead to negative predictions about specific performance or capability, such as, 'I'm sure I can't get the job done,' and to general beliefs about your competency and worth, such as, 'I'm just not very competent.'

Don't confuse confidence with dominance

Confidence is about being true to yourself and your values. Confidence is not about imposing your will and getting your own way.

Confident people tend to listen more than they speak, know the value of compromise and admit their mistakes. (Covering up mistakes burns up willpower, because your brain has to use precious energy to cloak errors.)

Disempowering pessimism

Negative beliefs can induce a pessimistic outlook that renders willpower irrelevant. After all, if you doubt your capability, you see little point in trying to do anything that may require willpower. Lacking confidence in yourself means that you waste the precious resource of willpower. On the other hand, if you can raise your level of confidence, your willpower can flourish.

The best way to exercise your willpower is by recognising what's important to express or achieve in any given situation, and deploying your willpower efficiently to that end.

Low self-confidence is also implicated in maintaining the state of learned helplessness referred to in the section 'Aiming for Realistic Optimism' earlier in this chapter. Negative expectations about your ability to cope or perform – for example, harbouring thoughts such as, 'I won't succeed, so I won't bother trying' or 'It's pointless' – obviously act as a barrier to progress. These beliefs can become self-fulfilling prophecies and trap you in a vicious circle.

In extremes, this type of pathological passivity resembles depression – the ultimate manifestation of hopelessness and apathy. More specifically, this mindset renders willpower redundant. After all, if you feel incapable of initiating action in pursuit of a personally relevant goal, you don't need willpower.

Even if you're feeling helpless, don't quit trying. You can lose your 'willpower fitness' as surely as the athlete who doesn't train for several weeks then gets breathless after running a few hundred metres. You should at least make an effort. Even if you don't succeed, you have at least learned something and exercised your willpower.

Boosting your self-confidence

You can train yourself to be self-confident.

Modelling – imitating someone else – is one of the most prevalent learning techniques. You pick up a huge range of behaviours through modelling – think of a little girl tottering around in her mummy's shoes or a little boy shoving his hands in his pockets and shrugging his shoulders just like his dad. Watching somebody, perhaps a person you admire and identify with, achieve what you want to accomplish can give you pointers on how to accomplish your own goals. The person need not be a personal friend: it may be a movie actor or comedian who bravely and publicly announced some problem or frailty, signalling that it's okay to be seen as vulnerable. Modelling is how most people learn how to do skilled jobs with confidence (although it's surely unfair to cite the trainee doctor's approach to medical procedures: see one, do one, teach one!).

In order to appear more confident when speaking to others, begin your sentences with 'I' rather than 'you'. For example, saying 'I'm frustrated that you're often late' is more direct than 'You frustrate me when you're late.' The second sentence sounds more accusing or even confrontational. It invites a more defensive, 'Well, I'm sorry you're frustrated, I'm just very busy these days!' or 'That's your problem, get over it,' rather than 'I didn't realise you felt that way.' The point is if you say, '*I* feel frustrated' the other person can't easily discount your feelings. As a result, punctuality is more likely in the long run, as is the survival of the friendship!

If you're unsure about committing to do something that may prove daunting, think of a good role model who has accomplished the task. It may be your favourite teacher who inspired you to give a good presentation, or the daytime television presenter who successfully quit smoking. By borrowing some of their self-confidence, you can boost your own – and your willpower as well.

Chapter 11

Creating a Lifestyle That Promotes Willpower

*M*anaging stress, acquiring good sleep habits, and embedding physical and mental exercise into your routine are the key ingredients of a lifestyle that promotes and sustains willpower. Lifestyle changes along these lines ensure that you can sustain your precious supply of willpower and remain resilient following setbacks.

Looking on the Bright Side

Along with good sleep, diet and exercise, one extra ingredient helps boost your willpower: acknowledging your success and celebrating your achievements. Recalling a successful, enriching or happy occasion can kick-start positive thinking, in the same way that remembering one bad outcome can lead to the recall of a cascade of calamities! The focus here is on the positive, however.

Try this exercise that entails recalling a rewarding, uplifting or joyous experience: every day for three successive days, spend 15 minutes writing about an intensely positive or rewarding experience you've had. You can start this exercise right away – you have permission to take a 15-minute break from reading this book!

This exercise can improve your health and happiness by broadening your experience of positive emotions and building your social networks and skills. It also helps you avoid getting trapped in what's been termed the *hedonic treadmill* – the constant search for new ways to find happiness and satisfaction.

The broaden-and-build approach, which you can foster by summoning up positive personal experiences, can enable you to build up personal resources that promote well-being and life satisfaction over extended periods of time. This, in turn, cultivates your willpower.

You don't learn or gain much by avoiding situations or experiences. Psychologists term this behaviour, which tends to be repetitive and stereotypical, *safety-seeking behaviour*. Approaching situations that entail meeting new people or gaining new experiences, on the other hand, stimulates your brain and can lead to more positive feelings. An active brain and a positive mindset can promote willpower.

Managing Stress

Stress saps willpower. In order to use willpower effectively you need to understand stress and how to manage it. Evolution has bequeathed you with a highly tuned system for responding to threats. In a crisis, this aids survival by giving you just three options, sometimes referred to as the three Fs: fight, flee or freeze. Note that reflection or cool deliberation is not part of the strategy in responding to what may be a matter of life and death. Historically, predators rarely gave a second chance, so these responses had to work rapidly and instinctively.

In modern society, you still occasionally rely on your survival instincts. For example, you jump out of the way of a speeding motorcycle.

But, usually, today's stressors are more chronic than acute, such as the threats posed by being made redundant at work, potential failure at an exam or the ending of a relationship. These threats, or worrying about them, can ratchet up your stress levels for months or even years. Our stress system is not best equipped to deal with these enduring stressors, but they look like they're here to stay!

Although you can't remove stress from your life, you can manage it better. And managing your stress, as I explain in in the next sections, is one of the most effective ways of maximising your willpower.

Perceiving and coping with stress

Stress is – as is said about beauty – in the eye of the beholder. *Stress* can be defined as a mental and physical state of arousal in response to a situation you perceive to be beyond your capacity to cope with.

Sometimes your perceptions are accurate. If you're told to double your productivity at work, for example, you experience stress, because this sounds like a tall order. Your perception that it's beyond your capacity is right (unless you're half asleep every day!). But if your boss says you have unrealised potential and can achieve much more, the situation is more ambiguous. In this scenario, you may experience self-doubt and perceive the demands as stressful and beyond your capacity. But you may also think that your ability has been recognised and rise to the challenge.

You can interpret such situations in different ways, and the interpretation influences how you predict the outcome and what your emotional response is. If the prediction overestimates the probability of a negative outcome (one of the common 'thinking biases' that emerge when you're confronted with uncertainty), the likelihood is that you'll become apprehensive, anxious or defensive. This emotional state can reduce your willpower, for example by focusing your attention on the signs and symptoms of anxiety or distress rather than the challenge posed by the task at hand. Ironically, this can lead to a self-fulfilling prophecy where a biased interpretation and negative prediction can distract you from performing at your best. The alternative is to aim for realistic optimism, meaning the best possible outcome in a given situation. (Check out Chapter 10 to discover more about realistic optimism.)

Asking 'Where's the evidence?'

I recently got a parking ticket. I'd parked on a quiet street near the river Thames in London on a Sunday afternoon when I thought parking was free.

When I saw the ticket on the windscreen, I immediately felt angry. My thoughts were 'I never get away with anything!' and 'I'm unlucky.' (I had some other thoughts as well, but the editor deleted my words!) When I calmed down, I remembered these thoughts and neither was in fact true: I'd escaped parking fines before, and, far from being unlucky, I've been fortunate in life. These thoughts nonetheless fuelled my anger – at the physical level creating the same state as stress, because anger activates the 'fight or flight' response.

The message is that if you're feeling stressed or angry, put your first thoughts aside and go to your second thoughts. A good way to gently challenge your thoughts is to ask yourself, 'Where's the evidence?' Left unchallenged, your first hot and angry thoughts can run away with you. A cooler, more reflective mindset is important to maximise your willpower. Research shows that sudden negative mood changes triggered by events such as receiving a parking ticket, losing your house keys or having an argument at work can undermine willpower.

The first step in overcoming a tendency to predict negative outcomes is to reflect on a situation where you acted more like a prophet of doom rather than a more balanced forecaster! This enables you to recognise negative thinking biases and replace them with more balanced predictions. You'll have more willpower available as a result. Try this:

1. **Recall a recent situation that you felt stressed about in advance.**

   It may have been a meeting at work, a job interview, a social gathering or simply a tedious journey.

2. **Write down your prediction about how you would experience the impending event and how stressed or anxious that made you feel.**

3. **Recall what actually happened.**

4. **Ask yourself whether the experience was as bad as you'd imagined it would be.**

Most likely, the situation entailed some nervousness at the beginning but was unlikely to match the scary expectations!

5. **Apply this method to a forthcoming event that you feel stressed about.**

   Are you 'awfulising' the event by imagining the worst case scenario?

Although things can and do sometimes go wrong, most people tend to overestimate the chances of this happening and how bad the situation would be if it did. This can make you stressed, deplete your willpower and, ironically, increase the chances of things going awry.

Depleting your willpower

Experiencing and reacting quickly to stressors or threats is essential for survival. However, prolonged exposure to high levels of stress can reduce your brain's efficiency in two ways:

- The worrying thoughts usually associated with stress draw energy away from your *willpower muscle* – the parts of the brain involved in planning and decision-making.

- Stress diverts mental energy away from the command-and-control centre of the brain – the seat of your willpower – and activates the more impulsive parts of your brain, called *hot-brain circuits*. Think back to the last time you were angry and swore – a typical example of a lack of will-power. My guess is that this was most likely when you were feeling stressed.

Connecting stress to performance

Experiencing some stress is inevitable, and indeed essential. If you're facing a particular challenge – for example preparing for a difficult exam or completing a complex project at work to a tight deadline – without some stress, you may not push yourself to study or to meet your deadline.

Figure 11-1 shows the relationship between performance and arousal or effort required. When you put in relatively little effort, your performance isn't particularly high. You're not placing demands on yourself, but neither are you being particularly productive. In order to perform better, you need to step up a gear or two. As the effort increases, requiring more willpower, so does performance. In due course, you reach the *optimal level of arousal* – the best compromise between effort and performance. Think of running, for instance. If you have to run 10 kilometres, your performance at any given time can be increased by going faster. But this means more arousal, with your heart, lungs and muscles all working harder. If you push too hard, your performance will decrease, perhaps requiring you to slow down or stop, so you need to balance the performance with what is a sustainable level of arousal or exertion, or you may not complete the circuit. Beyond this optimum level of arousal, as effort and associated stress levels continue to increase, performance can drop quickly.

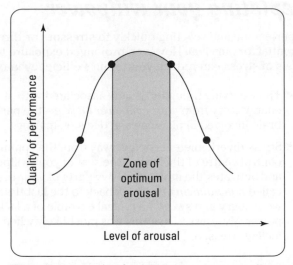

Figure 11-1: Achieving the right balance between effort and output.

The same principle applies to willpower. If you try to do too much too quickly – say, trying to complete several projects in the same timeframe – you may end up grinding to a halt like an exhausted jogger. You need to get the balance between sustainable effort and output right – your zone of the most efficient but sustainable performance.

Understanding the relationship between stress and performance can help you maximise and sustain your willpower. For example, if you realise that you're becoming stressed by a particular task, it's best to prioritise managing the stress by taking a short break to relax or meditate. High levels of stress compete with the demands of the task in hand for your limited supply of willpower.

Reacting to chronic stress

Your body and nervous system can adjust to acute or sudden stress very efficiently with no apparent ill effects (although you don't want nasty surprises too often!). However, in response to frequent or prolonged stress, your body releases hormones including the steroid cortisol. Cortisol can reduce the ability of your brain cells to maintain and repair themselves. This fact is meant to inform you, not alarm you: prolonged exposure to extreme stress is, fortunately, rare.

In many cases, the problem is that the stress is subtle, for instance linked to pressure to perform highly at work or to tension in a personal relationship. This hidden form of stress can undermine willpower by reducing your brain's fitness. The best way to counteract this is to monitor your levels of stress and find ways to de-stress or relax.

 Learning to relax doesn't require very much willpower in itself, and even short periods of relaxation can reduce stress levels. Physical exercise, socialising or just giving yourself five to ten minutes' breathing space can help you reduce stress.

Managing Your Mood with Food

I get grumpy when I'm hungry – or so I'm told! – and I'm pretty sure I'm not the only one who does. The grumpiness comes when levels of *serotonin,* regarded as a feel-good chemical messenger in the brain, drop. Serotonin is also involved in regulating appetite and sleep. Some of the most widely prescribed antidepressants appear to work because they help maintain or boost levels of serotonin. In turn, this enhances mood, regulates appetite and improves quality of sleep.

The right food, the right mood

The good news is that you don't need to take a pill to boost your levels of serotonin. Simply choosing the right foods and eating them at the right time will suffice.

Foods high in an amino acid known as *tryptophan* appear to increase the availability of serotonin in the brain. These foods include widely available items such as chicken, soya beans, tuna, tofu, spinach, asparagus and cow's milk – but only if the cow is fed on grass!

Sugar high, sugar low

Ingesting food or drink that contains high levels of sugar, such as processed, packaged meals and cola drinks, triggers a rapid increase in your blood sugar level followed by an equally sharp decline as your body produces insulin. This can cause fluctuations in your mood.

You can avoid these mood swings by choosing foods that release *carbohydrates* – organic compounds that change into sugar, or glucose, as you digest them – slowly. These foods are known as low glycaemic index (GI) foods. Table 11-1 contains examples of foods high and low on the index.

Table 11-1	Foods High and Low on the Glycaemic Index	
Category	*Low GI*	*High GI*
Fruits	Plums, apples, pears grapefruit	Watermelon, dates
Vegetables	Cauliflower, broccoli. cabbage, mushrooms, onions	Pumpkin, parsnips
Staples	New potatoes, pasta, brown rice	French fries, short grain white rice, instant mashed potatoes.
Breakfast cereals	Muesli, bran flakes (check for added sugar!)	Cornflakes, bran flakes

Visit www.the-gi-diet.org/lowgifoods for more information and a more comprehensive list of foods categorised by GI.

If you feel depressed to the point of despair, your sleep is chronically disturbed, you have a poor appetite and/or have thoughts of suicide, arrange to see your doctor or seek other professional support. Clinical depression is a complex disorder that requires careful assessment and specialist treatment.

Sleeping Your Way to Willpower

A good night's sleep helps you get the most from your willpower, but poor sleep, particularly if it's a regular occurrence, dilutes your willpower. Good-quality sleep also enables you to dream, because you need to attain a deep sleep state for this to happen. (If you've been deprived of sleep, you can dream much more quickly because you're in a state known as dream debt – you're owed some dream time!). Good-quality sleep, of sufficient duration to enable dreaming, helps you consolidate memories and process emotions. This can contribute to improved willpower.

Insomnia, defined as chronic difficulty in getting to sleep and staying asleep, can compromise your willpower. This is due to a *cognitive hangover,* like the unwelcome 'morning after' feeling but more to do with your thinking and mental functioning than the classic hangover syndrome.

Getting insufficient or disrupted sleep can compromise your willpower in two ways:

✔ It affects your mental concentration and short-term memory. Sustaining attention and remembering your goal and your motives are, of course, essential for willpower to be effective.

✔ It can make you more emotionally sensitive or reactive than usual – especially to potentially negative events. This reaction is a bit like a conventional hangover.

This creates a challenge from another angle as emotions compete for the same pool of mental energy as willpower. The willpower to resist the urge to express frustration or irritation, or to prevent yourself from nodding off at your desk, can't be used twice.

Recall one of the targets or goals requiring willpower that you set yourself, either in the past or perhaps while reading this book. Then, consider how insomnia-related tiredness may make it more difficult for you to generate and sustain willpower. If you experienced a setback or failure, what was your quality of sleep the night before? It may well be that your sleep was fine, but as nine out of ten people experience an occasional bad night's sleep, the information in this section may come in handy!

Even though insufficient or broken sleep can disrupt concentration, memory and emotional control the following day, your ability to make complex judgements and important decisions is usually not impaired. Your flexible brain can compensate for lapses in attention by temporarily increasing the power of your prefrontal cortex – the brain's CEO. Your brain needs to work harder, however, when it isn't sufficiently rested, and this effort may well prove to be exhausting.

Testing perceptions and having a plan

Jonathan was a successful website designer who worked from home and came to my psychology clinic after years of sleep problems. Typically, he would wake about an hour after falling asleep, remain awake for two to three hours, and sleep fitfully until it was time to get up to start work.

Anxiety about his work as a freelancer was one reason he couldn't sleep. He would then start worrying about the fact that because he wasn't able to sleep, he wouldn't be able to perform in his demanding job, and his livelihood would suffer.

As part of his treatment plan, Jonathan learned to reduce the frequency and intensity of his worrying, together with practising mindfulness meditation. However, while his sleep improved, he still worried about the consequences of not getting enough sleep. His belief was, 'If I don't get at least six hours' uninterrupted sleep, the quality of my work will be poor the following day.' We decided to explore this by means of a diary detailing his sleep and including a rating of his productivity and quality of work, including any feedback from customers. It emerged that while his sleep varied from poor to good, ranging from about four hours to six hours per night, there was no relationship between length of sleep and productivity or efficiency. In fact, he received excellent feedback from a customer about a website that he designed on a day following a rather poor night's sleep.

Insomniacs sleep more than they think they do! If you're a poor sleeper, you very likely unintentionally exaggerate the amount of time you're awake and minimise the time you spend sleeping. This is borne out by studies in specialist sleep laboratories where scientists can objectively measure the distinctive brainwaves associated with different stages of sleep. When the machines indicate, say, five hours' sleep, the insomniac guest may report an hour or less sleep. Think of it this way: you're bound to remember the periods of wakefulness more than the spells of, albeit interrupted, sleep.

Don't confuse tiredness and sleepiness. If you're tired, you can try resting or relaxing, but you may not be ready for bed quite yet. If you're showing signs of sleepiness – for example yawning, nodding off, rubbing your eyes – it's time to go to bed. You are, of course, usually likely to be tired when you feel sleepy. You're more likely to get to sleep quickly if you're both sleepy and tired.

Making Physical and Mental Exercise Routine

Inevitably, you already do physical and mental activities, so upgrading these into exercise shouldn't require too much effort or willpower. The difference between activity and exercise is that the latter is over and above your normal level of activity and is designed to stretch you physically or mentally. For example, you walk to the supermarket to do your shopping, but you run around the park to get fit.

Getting sufficient physical exercise

Remember that physical exercise benefits both body and brain fitness, so is the priority for willpower maintenance. Physical exercise is important at any age, but if you're over 50 or retired, your activity levels usually drop, so planned exercise is more necessary.

On a typical working day, I walk about five miles, simply getting to and from the train station and going from one clinic to another. This is often brisk walking, so qualifies as exercise rather than simply being active. If I wasn't working, I'd need to find other ways to exercise. I still aim to do aerobic exercise for 30 minutes to an hour, perhaps three times a week. Most regard this as an adequate level of physical exercise.

Exercising your brain

Brain fitness training isn't a case of one size fits all. If you're taking a degree course in a foreign language or doing a complex job (and most jobs are complex!), you're exercising your mental powers – often to the point of exhaustion. On the other hand, if you're unemployed or retired, you're less likely to be giving your brain a workout on a daily basis.

If you're in your 50s or older, you're likely to benefit more from mental exercise. This isn't all down to age, however. Older people's lifestyles can entail less novelty or challenge, perhaps because they've retired or are working part-time. Or maybe they're looking after an elderly relative, which calls for more routine than creativity. Younger folk may also be less mentally active or experience less novelty or challenge because they're unemployed. Accordingly, if you're less mentally active for any reason and/or older, it's especially important that you pursue mental activities that are novel, challenging and diverse. This helps maintain your brain's 'bandwidth' or capacity to process new information and solve new problems.

Visit `www.sharpbrains.com` to discover more about brain training. Mental exercise needn't involve being logged on to a computer. Social interaction and reading a novel with a complex plot give your brain a workout as well. In fact, one of the few activities that doesn't stretch your brain is watching television. Think about it!

Part IV

The Part of Tens

Enjoy an additional Part of Tens chapter online at www.
dummies.com/extras/willpower.

In this part . . .

✔ Pick up and take away ten key points about willpower to remember.

✔ Energise your efforts with ten ways to boost your willpower and achieve your goals.

✔ Further your knowledge and maintain your willpower with a little help from ten marvellous websites and apps.

Chapter 12

(More Than) Ten Things to Know about Willpower

*W*illpower defines humans as sentient, purposeful beings. No other creature has the mental machinery and motivation to keep a valued goal or dream alive for years, decades or perhaps a lifetime. Even when the inevitable occurs, we leave behind a set of instructions called a will to deal with our earthly possessions, ensuring that our willpower outlasts us – for the most part, that is, because where there's a will, there's a loophole, as the lawyers say!

Writing this book has taught me a lot about willpower, including my own fluctuating levels of the essential ingredient of getting anything done. In this chapter, my aim is to summarise and synthesise some of the key things I believe you should know about willpower.

For readers who've read most or all of the earlier chapters (well done you!), this chapter serves as a summary within which I accentuate key points. For those of you who, magpie-like, have been more selective (well done you, also: making decisions is good brain exercise, but don't overdo it!), reading this chapter ensures that you don't miss out on the core messages of the book.

Brain Fitness is Essential for Willpower

The human brain is the most complex organ in the universe. It evolved to this degree of complexity to enable simple capabilities: to start and maintain purposeful action and to stop or inhibit behaviour or impulses. A simplistic view, to be sure, but ultimately we are all stop-and-go creatures.

Your brain can conjure up immensely rich tapestries in order to fulfil its mission as your command and control centre. Your brain has evolved to construct mental maps of what the future might look like if you do one thing rather than another. This capacity to project into the future is one of the most important ways that your brain power supports your willpower. The most frequent challenge your willpower meets is deciding between a smaller, more immediate reward such as eating more, drinking more or logging on to that compulsive website, as opposed to envisioning the medium- to long-term future with fewer calories on board and greater productivity and success at work.

As I sit here, the thought of another cup of coffee arises. I then realise I've written only a few hundred words of the chapter, and make a deal with myself: another two hundred words and I'll make a cup of coffee. My brain, and your brain, is always brokering deals like this. Mundane though this bargain may appear, my brain has to do some work to keep me focused. The attractions of a short break and a cup of coffee have to be temporarily discounted and the value of the more distant goal of a completed chapter, and in due course the completed book, boosted.

Willpower emerges from the competition between conflicting goals and gratifications. In order to accomplish this complex balancing act, your brain needs to be structurally fit and well.

The importance of being match fit

Athletes distinguish between general fitness, in evidence during training, and *match fitness,* the ability to sustain high performance during actual competition. The latter places greater demands on your mental and physical resources.

Engaging your willpower to accomplish something, whether that entails stopping something compulsive or starting something difficult, places you in the competitive arena. Underlying deficiencies or weaknesses can be revealed when you're tested to extremes, so test and train your brain.

As an analogy, if you're planning to run a marathon, before you even consider a training regime, you check that you don't have a dodgy knee, or need a hip replacement, or experience chest pain on exertion. Similarly, before taxing your willpower, do your brain a favour by training it and nurturing it. It's a no-brainer! (Chapter 3 talks about ways to train your brain.)

The art of perseverance

Brain fitness, sometimes called *cognitive fitness,* is key to maximising your willpower. Imagine that you stopped smoking a week earlier. As you sit at your desk, perhaps feeling pressured by a work deadline, you crave a cigarette. You deal with this. But the longing comes back again 10 minutes later, and 20 minutes later, and so on. Each time, you have to perform mental gymnastics such as reminding yourself of the hazards of smoking and the benefits of being smoke free.

A fit brain can make a difference when you need to persevere. Switching back to the marathon analogy for a moment, imagine you're at the 15-kilometre mark alongside your training partner. But your partner hasn't been able to stick to the training regime and is beginning to flag. Because you're fitter, you carry on steadily. Fitness, whether you're testing your limbs or your brain through a willpower challenge, is the key to success.

You Can't Have a Willpower Bypass

Striving to exercise willpower is something everybody struggles with. Accepting the struggle helps you maintain confidence for the challenges to come. You can't have a willpower bypass – the statement, 'I have no willpower' is never true! Although everyone varies in the amount of willpower or self-control they can call on, to say, 'On that occasion, or with that particular behaviour, I lacked willpower' is truer.

If this book had an alternative title it would be *Managing Willpower For Dummies*. The key message is that, although willpower is one of your greatest personal assets, it needs to be trained, nurtured and cultivated. In a word, it needs to be managed. Part of this management process is recognising the limits of your willpower. (A book entitled *Infinite Willpower For Dummies* would be bought only by the naive and the gullible!)

Willpower never entirely disappears, but it can be overwhelmed if you take on too much or don't look after yourself. For example, if you've just moved house or started a demanding new job, it's probably not the best time to attempt to quit smoking or adopt that new diet.

Willpower Varies between People

Think of five people you know. They can be loved ones, friends, family, workmates, strangers in a queue (and how impatient they are!). Now rate them according to willpower. Expressions of low willpower can be impulsive actions such as spending too much, eating too much too often, not finishing things and being impatient or irritable. High willpower may be reflected in successfully quitting smoking, regulating diet and exercise, and generally finishing projects. Understanding why willpower varies from person to person can help you consolidate your strengths and mitigate your weaknesses.

Looking at the three reasons why willpower varies

What makes people differ in their willpower? The three main factors are genetics, past stress and current stress. I talk about each in the next sections.

Your genes

Your genetic code includes a set of instructions on how to build your brain (along with rest of you!). Some people's DNA, the language the instructions are written in, constructs brains that have strong brakes or strong connections to emotional or impulsive parts of the brain. This is the brain you need for maximum willpower. Other DNA patterns result in brain systems that are more emotional or impulsive, or have weaker connections to the control centre.

Willpower doesn't work equally for everything

Drawing on my experience working with people who've become addicted to alcohol and other drugs, I recently saw a man in his early 50s – I'll call him Paul – who was struggling to control his drinking. He told me that he'd achieved nine years of abstinence from alcohol, but started a pattern of excessive binge drinking once or twice a week for the previous year or so. He also told me (with justifiable pride!) that he'd quit smoking two years earlier, stating 'I have really good willpower.'

Clearly, Paul was able to show great resolve in some areas, but struggled with others. Depressed at not having a girlfriend, for example, he began to log on regularly to porn sites, even though he felt guilty while doing so.

Overall, the fact that he *believed* he had robust willpower, and had evidence to back this up such as quitting smoking and abstaining from alcohol for long periods, indicated to me that Paul would eventually gain control over other unwanted habits.

So willpower depletion can be seen as brake failure: your foot remains on the accelerator instead of the brake. Your goal is derailed, or at least off the road. Sounds familiar? Don't despair. This book aims to help you discover ways to increase your braking power – or your willpower; it's really much the same thing in many ways.

Exposure to stress in early life, or inconsistent parenting

Normal brain development is disrupted when basic needs aren't met in infancy and early childhood. This often happens because, sadly, a parent or *attachment figure* isn't present or available, is emotionally detached or even abusive. Being outside the home, at school or in the playground, can be a source of stress or unhappiness for a child in this situation. Unmet needs to be loved and to feel safe and protected can trigger a cascade of negative consequences.

In effect, the infant brain isn't able to develop to its full potential. For example, the ability to learn the self-control strategies at the core of willpower is disrupted because the child has to prioritise dealing with strong emotions evoked by feeling threatened or being harmed.

Current stress or challenge

The pressures, challenges or even traumas you experience in the here and now can drain your willpower.

A close friend was recently diagnosed with breast cancer (now fortunately treated and in remission). She became very distraught, and for more than two months was unable to make simple decisions, kept losing her keys, and was unable to control her emotions or her temper on occasion. Other goals such as redecorating and finding a new school for her little boy when he finished his primary education became insurmountable to this usually focused and competent person.

Obviously, my friend overcame far more than a failure of willpower, but her experience illustrates the fact that stress and trauma deplete your willpower. In the wake of many life experiences – the death of somebody close to you, an illness, the ending of a relationship – your willpower may seem to evaporate.

Managing the three reasons

Generally, unless you're affected by two or even three of the factors mentioned in the preceding sections, you won't have long-lasting problems with willpower.

You may, for argument's sake, be genetically less endowed with buckets of willpower (and the genetic question is indeed a complex scientific one, with much debate and controversy), but if you had loving parents or a good school, your willpower won't be affected in any real way. Equally, you may have had a difficult childhood but found happiness and contentment in later life.

The only factor you can't change is the genetic component. You can, however, manage your genetic predispositions. By way of illustration, if you're 6 foot 3 inches tall because you inherited the height gene, you'll do well to choose to live in a house with high ceilings! Similarly, if you seem to have inherited less rather than more willpower, you can develop strategies to manage this.

With regard to your life story, you can't rewrite history. While you can't erase your personal history or undo wrongs done to you, you can re-interpret or re-evaluate your past. This can help you achieve acceptance rather than blame or anger, emotions that can drain your willpower.

Focus is Your Friend

Distraction is the enemy of willpower, and focus is its friend. Staying focused on your goal helps your willpower flourish. The old saying 'the devil finds work for idle hands' could be rephrased as 'the devil finds distraction for idle minds'.

In the next sections, I describe complementary approaches to reduce the tendency for your mind to wander.

Find something that grabs your attention

Have you noticed that if you're bored you may start to day-dream, but if you're engrossed in a task you can forget to stop for lunch? That happens because your attention has spare capacity when you're stuck in a boring meeting but has nothing left to spare when you're 100 per cent focused on a task. In the latter scenario, you're less likely to detect triggers that compromise the pursuit of your goal.

For example, a colleague at work or a friend at a social event says, within earshot, 'I'm going for a cigarette.' Assuming that you've just quit smoking, if you have no spare capacity to notice or attend to this comment, you don't need to draw on your valuable supply of willpower to overcome the impulse to join in.

A distracter can come in any shape or form, depending on the goal you're engaging your willpower to achieve. The distracter may be noticing that the football game has just started on the sports channel when you're trying to write something. (This has just happened to me, even though I'm on the second floor in my study and the television is in the kitchen on the ground floor!) The game started 20 minutes ago, however, and I've only just noticed this because I was fully concentrating on the task in hand.

Practise mindfulness

Distraction is inevitable. There will be times when you have spare capacity in your attention system because you're obliged to carry out a tedious task that you find boring. If you're using willpower to overcome an appetite for food, sex, cigarettes or other drugs, this is where you need to be on your guard.

Mindfulness enables you to manage your wandering mind. In order to respond mindfully to unwelcome distractions or urges, you need to position yourself as a neutral observer. Simply notice that your attention has wandered in a direction at odds with your willpower. In the example of the sports channel, I noted without passing any judgement that my attention had indeed wandered away from my authorial duty. (I didn't say, 'I'm so easily distracted; will I ever finish this chapter?') I gently nudged my attention back onto my computer screen and writing the next paragraph.

Willpower Works on One Goal at a Time

A few weeks ago, I was on the London Underground after a meeting that had a long and complicated agenda. I was preoccupied with recalling the outcome of the meeting and what tasks the chair had assigned to me. When the doors opened at Embankment station, I shuffled out with some other passengers. The problem was, I should have stayed on until the next stop, Waterloo! To an observer, my behaviour looked entirely rational, but it was in fact unintentional and therefore devoid of willpower. My goal, to exit the train at Waterloo, was momentarily forgotten because I'd overloaded my *working memory* – the moment-to-moment guidance system we all have – by focusing on the meeting I'd attended. This occurred because I was juggling two competing goals at the same time: evaluating the outcome and implications of the meeting, and trying to get home. When I was distracted on the train, my willpower went walkabout for a moment, and led me to a premature exit. My willpower got me on the train, but I was soon on a different train of thought. This meant a few minutes delay.

You wouldn't get far in life if you literally did one thing at a time all day every day. Everyone has to multitask. The key point is that you need to recognise your limits – some people are better than others at juggling goals – and focus on one thing, moment by moment.

Clearly, you can entertain many goals at the same *approximate* time, but if these compete for willpower at the same critical moment, you may lose focus.

The magical number seven, plus or minus two

In 1956, George Miller wrote one of the most famous papers in psychology. In the paper, he described how most people can store between five and nine bits of information (seven plus or minus two) in short-term memory, which operates over seconds rather than minutes or hours. This short-term span applies to both visual and auditory information. So, whether you read or listen to, say a list of 20 types of plant, you'll be able to recall on average about seven.

More recently, researchers have concluded that this may be an overestimate or perhaps applies just to very simple tasks such as remembering objects or numbers. The magic number may in fact be as low as four, particularly if the chunks of information have to be manipulated or operated on, as in problem solving.

Momentarily forgetting your goal, especially if it is overcoming an appetitive urge, can lead to a lapse in willpower. If your willpower loses sight of your goal, it's of no use to you. With regard to willpower, the message is not to test or exceed your limits, whether you can store four or more bits of information. One way to do this is to focus on one goal at a time.

Tiredness Triggers Temptation

When you're tired, you're more likely to experience willpower failures. Try to balance your lifestyle and at least anticipate when you're likely to be exhausted, and then take steps to nurture your willpower – by aiming to get a good night's sleep, for example. When you're asleep, willpower is able to stand down, so think of sleep as one of the most important ways to cultivate your willpower. (Sleep is addressed in more detail in Chapter 11.)

If you do only one thing to create a good sleep–wake cycle, get up – and stay up and awake – at the same time each morning. This means weekends as well! The weekend lie-in, no matter how luxurious it feels, disrupts what experts call *sleep hygiene* – the routine or habits you develop to foster good regular sleep. If you sleep like a baby, you can probably ignore this, but remember it's easier to control the time at which you wake up than the time you fall asleep (at least for those who have sleep difficulties).

Hunger Zaps Your Willpower

When you're hungry, you're also more vulnerable to willpower failure. This is because using willpower requires an energy supply, especially in your brain. Your brain burns about 20 per cent of your glucose and over half of the oxygen in your blood. The more efficiently it does this, the more effective your willpower.

If you're dieting, your willpower is also focused on suppressing the urge to eat, which can result in depleting your willpower.

 Remember your motives! Remember your goal and the reasons you chose it. This is like giving yourself a pep talk. For example: 'I quit smoking and I intend to stay that way, because I want to become healthy and stay healthy.'

Keep Calm, or Get Calm, and Carry On

When you get upset, whether you're angry, anxious or depressed, your willpower tends to drain away. The mental resource needed to fuel willpower is diverted to dealing with the emotion.

 Ignoring emotions is like ignoring a red light on the dashboard. You need to address the emotion as a priority. This requires a lot of willpower to begin with, but prevents the emotion from draining willpower away.

You can respond to emotions in two ways. One is less helpful and entails ruminating or dwelling on the emotion in a negative way, for example thinking that you're so uncomfortable or stressed that you need to escape from the situation or change your mood by having a drink, smoking a cigarette or eating impulsively. This is like staring at the warning light on the dashboard and hoping it will stop flashing.

The second, more helpful, approach accepts the emotion, whether it's anxiety, anger or sadness – emotions that are familiar to everyone. Having recognised the emotion, the next step is to reflect rather than ruminate. Continuing the dashboard analogy, this may mean stopping the car and looking at the manual or even under the bonnet.

Reflection helps identify the underlying causes of problems or emotions ('When did I check the oil level in my car?' 'Did I take on too much work?' 'Did I avoid speaking up until the problem had become impossible to ignore?'). Gaining insight into the underlying causes can help you solve the problem. For example, if you identify a potential weakness in the boss's grand plan at work, you may decide that it's better to speak up sooner rather than later (be tactful – bosses have feelings too!). You can then explore ways to resolve the problem and then more is focused on the underlying problem.

Try new activities or rediscover former pastimes. Willpower is often called on when something is *removed* from your life – certain foods, alcohol, video games or social networking activities. Willpower can vanish into this gap if it's left unfilled! It's crucial to find new outlets and sources of reward or gratification when you generate change through willpower.

Cut Yourself Some Slack and Reward Yourself for Trying!

Be kind to yourself and respect the efforts you've made, even if you weren't able to sustain your willpower. Reward yourself for the effort you made, even if you don't achieve everything.

Maintaining a positive attitude is vital in maintaining your confidence and building resolve when you decide to face the next willpower challenge. Being optimistic is hoping for the best possible outcome, not the ideal outcome. If you wanted to lose five kilograms, lost three and put one back on, you're still winning. Moreover, you've learned the strengths and weaknesses of your willpower muscle.

Just Do Nothing: Give Your Brain a Rest

Surprisingly, just doing nothing isn't as easy as it sounds. It depends what you mean by 'doing nothing'. Your brain is always doing something, even when you're asleep. It's doing its own thing rather than striving to meet the demands you place on it using your willpower.

Here, by 'doing nothing' I mean nothing that requires willpower or physical effort. Sometimes, you just need to switch off. This gives your brain a rest – especially the circuits involved in sustaining willpower. A rested brain is able to deliver more will-power when it's online again.

In the resting state, your brain uses a little less energy (just five to ten per cent less, as measured by oxygen flow) compared with being active, but rest enables it to strengthen memories and connections between different networks, thus making your brain more efficient. For example, you process about a mega-byte of raw sensory information (think millions of megapixels!) through your eyes every second, so a chance to buffer and organise information is essential. It's easy: just shut your eyes! In the resting state your brain is also primed and ready for the next task. Think of a car engine that's idling: it's not using too much fuel but can quickly get going.

Plan for Failure, Find Success

A few years ago, when I had some savings, I put the money in a bank account that deducted interest every time I made a withdrawal. Frustrating? No! This made me happy, because *not* withdrawing money was what I wanted to do. I didn't just make a commitment, I made a pre-commitment. A *pre-commitment* is making a deal with yourself because you know that your will-power will fail at some stage.

Other examples of pre-commitments are:

- ✔ Not buying products that you know will challenge your willpower. These may be cigarettes, alcohol or chocolate in large quantities or as special offers (for example: get

50 per cent extra; buy one get one free; duty free goods when travelling). Note that you're imposing a potential cost on yourself by missing a bargain, but that's the whole point!

✔ Not buying tempting treats in the first place. This will give you time to react when you have cravings. Notice that you're using your cool, rational brain to guard against your impulsive 'I want' brain system. I call this strategic willpower.

✔ Telling friends, family and workmates that you're committing to your goal. The prospect of telling others you've had a setback can boost your motivation and encourage you to go the extra mile with your willpower.

Chapter 13

Ten Ways to Support Your Willpower

*F*rom eating well to getting good brain exercise, the tips in this chapter can help you boost your willpower and achieve your goals!

Eating a Breakfast of Willpower Champions

Start the day with a nutritious meal. Your brain has high energy demands, especially when it's using willpower to achieve something challenging or to suppress an unwanted habit.

 Eating a good breakfast is particularly important if you're aiming to lose weight by lowering your calorie count. Remember also to keep yourself replenished during the day; if you're hungry, you're primed to seek high-calorie foods that have less fuel for your willpower. And remember that if you're too strict with your diet, or choose sugary foods that just provide temporary respite from hunger, you end up with more calories and less willpower.

Training Your Brain

Practise discreet brain training! Keeping your brain sharp is essential for maximising your willpower, as I describe in detail in Chapter 3. Fortunately, even when you're stuck in a boring meeting, where fiddling with your smartphone or using a pen and paper to do brain exercises is definitely uncool, your thoughts and mental processes remain silent and invisible to others!

You can use this to your advantage by giving your brain a silent workout. This could be through using a memory game. For example, try to recall every city you've visited and the names of the hotels you stayed in. You can extend this to recalling the name of each country's political leader or head of state. A rather more creative approach to covert brain training is to challenge yourself to generate as many words as you can beginning with a particular letter such as F, A or S, in a minute. Or you can think of names of animals, plants, modes of transport, musical instruments. In fact, coming up with a list of possible categories such as this is itself a creative process! It may seem simplistic, but exercise of this type activates key parts of your brain involved in creativity and memory.

If you're doing this brain training at work, use your judgement and don't get carried away! You can, however, safely rely on the *cocktail party effect*. This isn't a happy hour at the nearest bar, but a psychological term for your ability to quickly detect meaningful words such as your name or other personally relevant information even when you're not tuned in to others' conversations. These words can instantly grab your attention as you focus on an armadillo or a zebra!

De-cluttering Your Personal Space

Untidy or cluttered worktops, desktops or rooms can be distracting and make things difficult to find – both of which can deplete your willpower. Every distraction means that you have to deploy willpower to refocus. Not finding things can also cause frustration or distraction, which is another tax on your precious willpower.

I recently started the de-cluttering process, beginning with my CD collection. For two years or more I've been listening to streaming music through a Wi-Fi service. There wasn't even a CD player in the room! Still, placing my once-precious collection of CDs in a cardboard box was difficult, and I couldn't bear to actually dispose of them. Nonetheless, the soundtrack of my youth is now safe in my spacious cellar, and my living room has less clutter and more feng shui.

So, when you finish this chapter, look around your house and consider getting rid of any clothes, gadgets and anything else taking up space and gathering dust. Note that this suggestion is in the form of an *implementation plan*. I'm not suggesting that you do it when you get around to it (perhaps never!), but at a particular point: '*When* I finish this chapter *then* I'll de-clutter one room or one part of one room.' (I talk about implementation strategies in Chapter 6.)

Knowing what You're Drinking

When shopping for alcoholic beverages in the supermarket or an off licence, always check the percentage of alcohol in the product, known as the alcohol by volume (ABV) index. At first glance, the difference between a beer that's five per cent ABV and one that's four per cent ABV seems minimal. Surely, a one per cent difference doesn't matter. But it does! The higher-rated product is actually 25 per cent higher in alcohol! Thus a litre of the stronger product contains five standard units (each unit is about 10 grams of pure alcohol) compared with the four per cent ABV beer, which contains four standard units.

Always have a glass of water at hand when drinking wine with your meal (or without a meal!).

Managing Your Anger

Make an effort to manage your anger or frustration before trying to resolve any conflicts at home or at work. If you're feeling angry towards somebody you know, you're likely to say the wrong thing, because your willpower is compromised. Moreover, anger is often expressed towards those entirely blameless, such as friends and family or other drivers who innocently meander too close to your vehicle!

Planning Your Shopping

Shop in places where you know you'll have fewer impulses to buy items you don't want to spend money on. If you're cutting down on your alcohol consumption, don't stroll down the street that has a pub at each corner. If your goal is to lose weight, avoid the gourmet cheese shop.

And, especially if you're using willpower to rein in your spending habits, shopping smart is a must. The mental effort you use to keep within your budget can actually exhaust your willpower, and you can end up spending more than you can afford. That's why tempting treats like glossy magazines and confectionary are placed near the till.

Using a shopping list is an excellent way to conserve willpower and control impulsive shopping. From the willpower perspective, the shopping list spreads the workload. The decisions about what to buy are made in advance, perhaps when you're sitting in your kitchen enjoying a cup of coffee. These decisions require willpower, but you use your cool reflective brain system to do what it's best at: making rational decisions, unhindered by the triggers drawing you to items you want rather than need.

With a list in hand as you traverse the aisles of the supermarket, you place fewer demands on your willpower because you have fewer decisions to make. You therefore have more willpower capacity to resist the impulse buys when your willpower begins to wane after 30 or 40 or more minutes of shopping.

Prioritising Your Resolutions

Make one New Year's resolution, or commit to one specified goal at any time of the year, and stick to it! Work out your priorities and choose one important goal. With willpower, success fosters success, so achieving one objective strengthens your willpower muscle. Striving for more than one goal dilutes your willpower and compromises success on all fronts.

Ask yourself what your priorities are. Quitting smoking may be more important that losing weight. Keep in mind that succeeding with one goal gives you more confidence when you take on the next challenge.

Being Assertive Rather Than Submissive or Confrontational

Practise being assertive: biting your lip and suppressing your feelings repeatedly exhausts your supply of willpower. A strong link exists between submissiveness, or not sticking up for yourself, and subsequent experience of and expressions of anger.

However, being assertive doesn't mean you should go on a mission of zero tolerance of minor slights or acts of thoughtlessness by others! Try to balance assertiveness with empathy and understanding and avoid the double-standards trap, whose technical name is *attributional bias,* in which you assign causality or blame in a self-serving manner. This bias leads you to account for your own errors by emphasising the influence of external factors such as being poorly managed or acquiring too many duties at work, but attributing the failures of other people to internal or personal characteristics such as being disorganised, incompetent or, perish the thought, lacking willpower! Be fair to yourself, but also be fair and compassionate to others.

Even if your anger is justified, heightened negative emotion places ultimately unnecessary demands on your willpower. Remember the Buddhist saying, 'You will not be punished for your anger, you will be punished by your anger.'

Tackling Your Problems Stepwise

Break complex problems into smaller and more manageable steps. Instead of, say, setting a goal of branching out into a new career, decide to update your CV and send it to a recruitment agency. Or identify a core skill or qualification that could mobilise your career.

Willpower works when it's directed at one goal at a time. Spreading your willpower too thinly is likely to lead to not quite making it on a number of fronts rather than succeeding on one. Willpower works better sequentially rather than in parallel.

Being Optimistic but Realistic

Don't assume that things will be more difficult than they prove to be, or that the difficulties that arise will prove to be insurmountable. The notion that I describe in more detail in Chapter 10 is *realistic optimism,* which forecasts the best possible realistic outcome given the circumstances.

A pessimistic or negative outlook rapidly deflates willpower. It simply makes willpower irrelevant, because effort seems pointless in pursuit of a negative outcome.

Chapter 14

Ten (Plus) Willpower-related Websites and Apps

In This Chapter

▶ Using online resources to boost your willpower

▶ Finding apps to keep you focused, relaxed and happy

▶ Keeping your brain and body fit

▶ Making humour a willpower tonic

*T*he Internet, and apps available through it, can help you maintain and boost your willpower in a variety of creative ways. You can also use the Internet to follow your own interests in the broader cultural arena; for example, you can make a virtual visit to many of the world's leading galleries and museums, or listen to virtually any genre of music. Make use of the tools here and explore for more.

Using Smartphone Apps

Your smartphone can be your willpower's best friend, or at least its steadfast supporter. You just need to ensure that the battery remains charged or can be topped up! A smartphone or other electronic device can offer the following aids to willpower:

✔ Remind you of your goal by sending alerts.

✔ Provide a discreet way to monitor almost any behaviour related to habits, diet or lifestyle.

✔ Provide feedback regarding progress and achievements.

✔ Give encouragement and reinforcement. (I just received a message about my weekly exercise session, telling me 'Well done Frank, you kicked butt this week!')

✔ Allow you to exercise your brain while on the move.

✔ Facilitate meditation and relaxation programmes.

✔ Make it easy for you to maintain and build your social networks. Friends and family can be 'cheerleaders', encouraging you when your willpower wavers.

✔ Entertain and amuse you with music, videos, books or games when you need to divert yourself from a trigger.

✔ Enable you to monitor the duration and quality of your sleep.

In addition to the specific help or guidance a smartphone app can provide, you are in a way outsourcing some of the work your willpower needs to do in maintaining vigilance and control. This aligns with the consistent theme of this book: willpower can be a very powerful resource that needs to be nurtured and conserved in order for it to be available when you really need it. If you can rely on an app or program to remind and motivate yourself, you'll have more mental energy when you need it – more of what psychologists call *cognitive reserve.*

Keeping Your Brain Fit with SharpBrains

The website www.sharpbrains.com is a one-stop shop for brain fitness. Maintaining optimal brain fitness in order to foster willpower is the most important message in this book.

If you choose only one of the many resources listed in this chapter, I suggest you read *The SharpBrains Guide to Brain Fitness,* written by Alvaro Fernandez, Elkhonon Goldberg and Pascale Michelon and available through the SharpBrains website. The first edition proved to be an invaluable source to me as an author, and the recently published second edition is even better. I've also heeded the clear evidence-based advice on diet, exercise and lifestyle.

SharpBrains hasn't yet developed an app, but you can register to receive weekly newsletters as well as follow it on Twitter or Facebook.

Recording Your Goals with GoalWriter

Giving your goal a prominent position in your working memory – on your brain's desktop – is by far the most effective way to stay focused, avoid distraction, and overcome temptation. The free tools at www.goalwriter.com enable you to do just that. They guide you to identify your mission, your vision and your values. You can also focus on your strengths and weaknesses as well as the opportunities and threats that may impact on your success in attaining your goals – a process known as SWOT analysis.

Importantly, if you forget to log on to review or update your progress, you receive an email alert. These automatic email alerts mean you don't have to assign precious willpower to reminding yourself to carry out the particular task. Anything that conserves willpower is a good thing. It is also free to register and use GoalWriter, so as well as being light on willpower, it's light on your pocket!

GoalWriter doesn't appear to have an app that you can use on your smartphone or tablet, but other apps such as MyEffectiveHabits (which you can find at https://play.google.com/store/apps/details?id=com.andtek.sevenhabits&hl=en), Goal Coach (available at https://play.google.com/store/apps/details?id=com.bluewave.goaltracker&hl=en) and The Habit Factor (offered via the www.thehabitfactor.com/welcome website) are available. Typically, the apps come in a free version with the option of paying a small amount for more-advanced or user-friendly functions.

Dieting with the Beck Diet Solution

The www.beckdietsolution.com website is excellent, as is the sourcebook *The Beck Diet Solution: Train Your Brain To Think Like a Thin Person* by Dr Judith Beck. This is one of the few books about diet that focuses on the dieter rather than the food. It applies the powerful techniques of cognitive therapy to help you regulate your eating in the long term. As Dr Beck states, no effective short-term diet exists; the benefits of dieting and associated lifestyle change can only be judged in the long term.

The website offers a large range of resources. You can follow the Beck Diet Solution on Twitter or Facebook or subscribe to the newsletter. An app called Diet Assistant enables you to choose healthy options for breakfast, snacks, lunch and dinner. Diet Assistant also provides information on low glycaemic index foods which release glucose slowly and are the best way to fuel your brain in order to sustain willpower.

Monitoring Your Physical Exercise

Exercising a few times a week is a proven means of maintaining a healthy brain and is essential for promoting willpower. Technology has really come up with some brilliant solutions here. The best approach is using a small portable movement monitor (such as Fitbit www.fitbit.com or Jawbone www.jawbone.com) that captures every step you take (or even every move you make!). These apps and devices can also be used to monitor your sleep in terms of duration and quality. Additionally, a Fitbit bracelet can also be programmed to operate as a silent alarm. (The first time I used it, unfortunately I forgot I'd set the alarm, and was quite startled to feel something vibrating on my arm at 7 a.m.!)

With these technological solutions, you get real-time feedback about your efforts, which is a great boost your willpower and motivation. You can also set daily or weekly targets, which ticks the all-important goal-setting box vital for willpower. Using technology to outsource mental effort and preserve willpower, these systems require little or no willpower once you start using them. A case of 'Fitbit and forget', which frees up your willpower for other uses.

Training Your Brain

Because your brain is, in effect, a universal or multipurpose computer, any activity, mental or physical, activates it. In order to be effective at increasing mental efficiency, you need to do mental exercise, which means doing something new. New activities entail effort and thereby challenge your brain to work harder. Here, I divide mental exercise into general or global pursuits that draw on a whole range of cognitive function on the one hand, and more specific approaches to particular functions like attention and memory on the other hand.

Generic brain training

As the heading indicates, this type of brain training can be anything that entails new learning or discovery, often with the help of online resources or apps. Examples include:

- ✔ Learning a new language
- ✔ Reading a novel, biography or other text that requires sustained concentration and memory
- ✔ Learning a new musical instrument
- ✔ Taking an online education course
- ✔ Signing up for (and completing!) an evening class in anything from aromatherapy to zoology
- ✔ Building or consolidating your presence and connections on social networking sites

Specific brain training

The main finding is that practice with any particular game that involves memory or attention skills leads to improvement with the game. Although scores improve, however, much less evidence exists that this improvement generalises to other activities involving work or study. (*The SharpBrains Guide to Brain Fitness* offers a comprehensive review of the efficacy of brain training games and apps.)

Because working memory is so important for effective willpower, I suggest that training that boosts this ability to store and manipulate information in the short term is the priority.

An app called the n-back enables you to practise boosting working memory capacity. The task requires you to process strings of letters or numbers. Stimuli (numbers or letters) are presented in a sequence, and you're required to recall repetitions such as 6, **8**, 7, **8**, **5**, 3, **5**, where *n* represents the number of steps back in the sequence you have to go. In the example, *n* = 2, and the correct responses are 8 and 5, because they were not the previous number but the second previous number. An n-back test where *n* = 1 would be much easier, because you'd only have to repeat the preceding number. You can see a demonstration of the n-back on `http://cognitivefun.net/test/4`. With practice, you can increase *n* to three or four. This isn't easy, but is a great way to increase the stamina of your working memory, the central processor of willpower.

Brain Metrix at `www.brainmetrix.com` also has a broad range of resources you can use to enhance your brain's efficiency and hence your willpower.

Brain training, especially when requiring strenuous effort, depletes your willpower in the short term while promising to augment it in the longer term. Choose the time you practise carefully: perhaps not in the middle of a very busy working day, but on an occasion when you have a chance to recharge your willpower battery. Recalling that willpower can be regarded as a mental muscle, if you plan to run a marathon, you wouldn't run ten miles before that to warm up!

Managing Your Mood

Negative mood states soak up your vital willpower like a sponge. Some excellent resources are available to help you manage your mood and preserve your willpower:

- ✔ Living Life to the Full (`www.llttf.com/index.php`) is a well-resourced site designed to help you identify and manage negative moods and promote psychological well-being.

- ✔ The MoodGYM (`http://moodgym.anu.edu.au/welcome`) is devoted to helping people with depression, through cognitive behaviour therapy.

- ✔ About.com's stress management page (`http://stress.about.com/od/tensiontamers/a/exercises.htm`) has a particular focus on mindfulness and relaxation tools.

- ✔ Cognitive Behaviour Therapy Self-Help Resources at `www.getselfhelp.co.uk` has an impressive range of resources that can help you develop willpower.

✔ MoodPanda app (www.moodpanda.com), which I recommend for monitoring your mood discreetly.

Simply recognising and labelling your emotions, particularly if they're on the negative side, helps you gauge how much willpower you may be able to summon up. If you realise that you're stressed or feeling a bit down, you can address your emotional state before embarking on an activity that will challenge your willpower. MoodPanda helps you do this. This makes it more likely that you'll preserve your supply of willpower for use when you don't have to struggle with unruly emotions.

Finding Mindfulness and Meditation

Meditation is a proven means of sustaining and improving willpower. Meditation practice teaches you how to control your attention, which is essential to sustaining willpower, because distraction and temptation are two formidable foes. In addition, meditation improves your sense of well-being and fosters spiritual growth. These are the ingredients of a lifestyle that supports willpower.

Numerous websites and apps guide you and encourage you to practise meditation. I like Buddhist Meditation Trainer, a free app that you can find at https://play.google.com/store/apps/details?id-com.bmt&hl=en_GB. The free Mindfulness Bell app (https://play.google.com/store/apps/details?id=com.googlecode.mindbell&hl=en_GB) is a simple but elegant way to remind you to take a step back and reflect mindfully in the course of a busy day. For more intensive work on meditation, visit www.buddhistrecovery.org. As indicated by the website's title, the site is aimed at people who have had significant problems with addictions or compulsions. It offers some very good resources.

Some years ago, I attended a workshop by Jon Kabat-Zinn, who has devoted his life to promoting the practice of mindfulness meditation as a means of promoting well-being and health. Again and again he emphasised that meditation needed to be done regularly, at least on a daily basis.

Like willpower, meditation can be compared to a muscle that grows stronger with practice.

Overcoming Harmful Habits

Habits are a big challenge to overcome because they have long memories that can take advantage of lapses in willpower. Useful sites include:

- ✔ www.quit.org.uk: Excellent resources and advice for quitting smoking.

- ✔ www.downyourdrink.org.uk: Useful for reducing or moderating your alcohol intake if you think it has crept up to a level that may be affecting your health, relationships and productivity. As well as being a problem in its own right, excessive drinking can be detrimental to willpower.

- ✔ www.gamblingtherapy.org: This website offers telephone and online advice for people anywhere in the world concerned about their gambling behaviour. (A declaration of interest here: this is run by a charity called the Gordon Moody Association, of which I am a trustee.)

- ✔ www.talktofrank.com: This site offers accurate evidence-based advice on the full spectrum of drugs that are liable to be abused. (No declaration of interest here; it just happens to include my name!)

Improving Your Well-being with Authentic Happiness

Willpower flourishes in the context of well-being. The website www.authentichappiness.com is, as its name suggests, focused on promoting realistic optimism. (I address the concept in Chapter 10.) The pursuit, and hopefully attainment of, authentic happiness is a willpower investment that returns great dividends.

Success breeds success: you're more likely to reach out to others and be more creative if authentic happiness comes your way. Everything seems a bit easier if you're feeling happy. Your brain actually works better when it isn't burdened by negative emotions and instead can reach out to achieve its full potential – or, more accurately, your full potential!

Having a Laugh

I'm serious! Laughter is good for you and your willpower, so laugh a lot (even if you have to laugh at yourself). Laughter appears to be an antidote to stress and also helps you adopt a new perspective, perhaps giving you some ideas for solving a problem (but let's not get serious again!).

You can choose from a wide selection of humour apps and websites. I don't recommend any particular one, because I think humour is subjective. Try search terms such as 'humour' or 'laughter' and you'll be spoiled for choice. I warn you that some sites can be rude or risqué, and some of the jokes have been around the block not once but many times!

Try finding your favourite clips from the sitcoms that used to make you laugh heartily. Laughter is a true tonic for your willpower.

Index

Notes

Notes

Notes

About the Author

Frank Ryan is a consultant clinical psychologist and cognitive therapist working in the National Health Service in London, UK. He is also an Honorary Senior Lecturer in the Division of Brain Sciences, Department of Medicine, at Imperial College, London. The focus of his research is behavioural and cognitive processes in impulse control. He is the author of *Cognitive Therapy for Addiction: Motivation and Change* (Wiley-Blackwell, 2013).

Author's Acknowledgements

I would like to thank Claire Ruston, Rachael Chilvers and Steve Edwards. They all contributed to this book at various stages from commissioning to editing and, ultimately, publication. In truth, they provided me with the support and guidance that is essential for willpower to flourish. I also want to gratefully acknowledge the diligence of the development editor, Kathleen Dobie, and the proofreader, Mary White. I am deeply indebted to the many talented researchers and fellow authors whose work forms the basis of much of this book. Thanks are also due to the many people who have come my way in my clinics, who have taught me so much about willpower and how it can ultimately transform lives.

Dedication

To Roz, with love.

Publisher's Acknowledgements

We're proud of this book; please send us your comments at http://dummies. custhelp.com. For other comments, please contact our Customer Care Department within the U.S. at 877-762-2974, outside the U.S. at (001) 317-572-3993, or fax 317-572-4002.

Some of the people who helped bring this book to market include the following:

Acquisitions, Editorial and Vertical Websites

Project Editors: Rachael Chilvers, Steve Edwards

Development Editor: Kathleen Dobie

Commissioning Editor: Claire Ruston

Assistant Editor: Ben Kemble

Copy Editor and Proofreader: Mary White

Publisher: Miles Kendall

Cover Photo: ©iStockphoto.com/ Bartosz Hadyniak

Project Coordinator: Sheree Montgomery

Take Dummies with you everywhere you go!

Whether you're excited about e-books, want more from the web, must have your mobile apps, or swept up in social media, Dummies makes everything easier.

Visit Us

Like Us

Follow Us

Watch Us

Join Us

Pin Us

Circle Us

Shop Us

FOR DUMMIES

A Wiley Brand

BUSINESS

978-1-118-73077-5

978-1-118-44349-1

978-1-119-97527-4

MUSIC

978-1-119-94276-4

978-0-470-97799-6

978-0-470-49644-2

DIGITAL PHOTOGRAPHY

978-1-118-09203-3

978-0-470-76878-5

978-1-118-00472-2

Algebra I For Dummies
978-0-470-55964-2

Anatomy & Physiology
For Dummies, 2nd Edition
978-0-470-92326-9

Asperger's Syndrome For Dummies
978-0-470-66087-4

Basic Maths For Dummies
978-1-119-97452-9

Body Language For Dummies,
2nd Edition
978-1-119-95351-7

Bookkeeping For Dummies,
3rd Edition
978-1-118-34689-1

British Sign Language For Dummies
978-0-470-69477-0

Cricket for Dummies, 2nd Edition
978-1-118-48032-8

Currency Trading For Dummies,
2nd Edition
978-1-118-01851-4

Cycling For Dummies
978-1-118-36435-2

Diabetes For Dummies, 3rd Edition
978-0-470-97711-8

eBay For Dummies, 3rd Edition
978-1-119-94122-4

Electronics For Dummies
All-in-One For Dummies
978-1-118-58973-1

English Grammar For Dummies
978-0-470-05752-0

French For Dummies, 2nd Edition
978-1-118-00464-7

Guitar For Dummies, 3rd Edition
978-1-118-11554-1

IBS For Dummies
978-0-470-51737-6

Keeping Chickens For Dummies
978-1-119-99417-6

Knitting For Dummies, 3rd Edition
978-1-118-66151-2

FOR DUMMIES®

A Wiley Brand

SELF-HELP

Cognitive Behavioural Therapy DUMMIES

978-0-470-66541-1

Creative Visualization DUMMIES

978-1-119-99264-6

Mindfulness DUMMIES

978-0-470-66086-7

LANGUAGES

Spanish DUMMIES

978-0-470-68815-1

Polish DUMMIES

978-1-119-97959-3

British Sign Language DUMMIES

978-0-470-69477-0

HISTORY

The Tudors DUMMIES

978-0-470-68792-5

Medieval History DUMMIES

978-0-470-74783-4

British History DUMMIES

978-0-470-97819-1

Laptops For Dummies 5th Edition
978-1-118-11533-6

Management For Dummies,
2nd Edition
978-0-470-97769-9

Nutrition For Dummies, 2nd Edition
978-0-470-97276-2

Office 2013 For Dummies
978-1-118-49715-9

Organic Gardening For Dummies
978-1-119-97706-3

Origami Kit For Dummies
978-0-470-75857-1

Overcoming Depression
For Dummies
978-0-470-69430-5

Physics I For Dummies
978-0-470-90324-7

Project Management For Dummies
978-0-470-71119-4

Psychology Statistics For Dummies
978-1-119-95287-9

Renting Out Your Property
For Dummies, 3rd Edition
978-1-119-97640-0

Rugby Union For Dummies,
3rd Edition
978-1-119-99092-5

Stargazing For Dummies
978-1-118-41156-8

Teaching English as a Foreign
Language For Dummies
978-0-470-74576-2

Time Management For Dummies
978-0-470-77765-7

Training Your Brain For Dummies
978-0-470-97449-0

Voice and Speaking Skills
For Dummies
978-1-119-94512-3

Wedding Planning For Dummies
978-1-118-69951-5

WordPress For Dummies, 5th Edition
978-1-118-38318-6